The Ultimate Book of

RUDE
AND
POLITICALLY
INCORRECT
JOKES

The Ultimate Book of

RUDE
AND
POLITICALLY
INCORRECT
JOKES

ALLAN PEASE

PORTICO

First published in Great Britain in 2001

This edition published in 2008 by
Portico
10 Southcombe Street
London
W14 0RA

An imprint of Anova Books Company Ltd.

ISBN 9781861054494

A CIP catalogue record for this book is available from the British
Library.

20 19 18 17 16 15 14 13 12

Printed and bound by CPI Mackays, Chatham, Kent, ME5 8TD

Send complaints or abuse to allan@dontcare.com

This book can be ordered direct from the publisher at
www.anovabooks.com

ACKNOWLEDGEMENTS

I can't recall when most of the jokes in this book were told or by whom, but here's a list of those who personally told me some of the most memorable or made me laugh the hardest.

Anita Kite, Barbara Pease, Barry Markoff, Terry Butler, Mike Goldring, Ben Gaze, Ray & Ruth Pease, Graham Dufty, Bert Newton, Kerri-Anne Kennerley, Max Walker, Rosanna & Simon Townsend, Frank Boggs, Rob Edmunds, Dave & Jan Goodwin, Alex & Denise McTaggart, Lenny Henry, Esther Rantzen, Bernard Croft, Sally Jesse-Raphael, Diana Ritchie, Bill Suter, Martin Grunstein, John Tickel, Bob Johnson, Sheri MacRae, Daryl Somers, Peter Draper, Peter Kay, Ron Tacchi, Amanda Gore, Ronnie Corbett, Paula Thompson, Jo Fenwick, John Fenton, Dick Byrne, Roger Dawson, Jim Cathcart, Doc Blakely, Robert Henry, Jack Levi, Max Hitchins, Melissa Pease, Jasmine Pease, Adam Sellars, Gary Skinner, Allan & Anne Parker, Andy Clarke, Raelene Hall, Errol Hibberd, John Macintosh, Bob Geldof, Kamahl, Gay Byrne, Pat Kenny, Don Lane, Ernie Sigley, Denise Drysdale, Nick Owen, Rob Miller, Dennis Waitley, Richard Otton, Iven Frangi, Christine Maher, Leanne Harrison, Chris Ganderton, Michael Pease, Peter & Pat Walsh, Roger Varney, Fat Wilson, John Allinson, Mike Creagan, Bob McLennan, Trevor Otton, Doug & Peter Bailey, Uli Huber, Graeme Shiels, Ron Barassi, Graham White, Derek Morris, Chris Fenton, Cliff Ritchie, Frank Todisco, Nellie Carter, Alan Francis, Tom Manwarring, Steve Harris, Steve Foy, David Hunt, Ian McKay, Gordon Cramer, Kevin Austin.

DEDICATION

To the Peases who, in helping organise and compile this volume, have learned the art of being Rude and Politically Incorrect.

INTRODUCTION

Picture this scene:

Julius Caesar walks to the podium to address the senate on the state of the Empire. As he begins his address, a senator sitting near the back leans across to two other senators and says "You know, Caesar's parents nearly lost him as a child. Unfortunately they didn't take him far enough into the desert."

The three burst into laughter ... "and you can tell when he's lying – his lips are moving!" chides another. Now, 6 of them are sniggering, trying not to be obvious. But Julius is unimpressed. That night, they are thrown to the lions for being Politically Incorrect.

So who told the first jokes? I've heard those same lines used against politicians in most countries as I travel the world giving seminars. And most of the joke-tellers think they've got new or original jokes, yet jokesters were being put to death thousands of years ago for cracking the *same* lines.

I give around 150 seminars and speeches a year and travel to over 30 countries and I reckon I've heard just about *every* joke there is. It's even hard for me to find a new one on the Internet. Whilst I'll take credit for a few original jokes, this book is a collection of the best ones I heard from friends, relatives, neighbours, business associates, clients and conference delegates – but there are few *new* jokes. It usually takes a terrible disaster like a military coup, mass murder, earthquake or plane crash to give birth to new humour. When the NASA space shuttle exploded there was an abundance of new material being told the **next** morning. "What does NASA stand for? Need another seven astronauts." "NASA's new advertisement – Become an Astronaut – Go Up as a School Teacher, Come Back as a Marine Biologist." "What colour were the Astronaut's Eyes? Blue – one blew to the left, the other blew to the right." I heard these jokes the morning after the disaster as I boarded a plane in Sydney heading for London. When I arrived at Heathrow, my host told me *exactly the same jokes*. This was at a time when the only way of spreading jokes quickly was by phone or telex!

The jokes in this book are politically incorrect, rude or both. I've omitted crude jokes or anything that I considered gross, slanderous or obscene because you don't need it to be funny. (Obscene is anything that gives the judge an erection.) Most of the humour here deals with attitudes or choices – gays, lesbians, public servants, lawyers, sexists, feminists, discrimination, attitudes, farters, bankers and wankers.

Lawyers and religious nuts get an extra large serve here. Lawyers because everyone loves lawyer jokes and religion because, as a kid, I had the Catholic Church forced down my throat for years. As a 6-year-old, I wanted to be an altar boy – but I'd be buggered if I'd be one now. Thanks to bishops, vicars and priests everywhere dropping their drawers and playing hide-the-sausage, the Church has become a deserving butt of ridicule.

How do you make a nun pregnant?

Dress her up as an altar boy.

A priest told me that one.

Sometimes I'm called sexist. It's usually by a feminist. For these women, sexism is anything a man says or does. My wife Barbara will tell you I'm the least sexist man around. When we first met we had a fast and furious affair – I was fast, she was furious.

So how do you remember jokes? Simple – when you hear a good one, write it down. For twenty years I wrote them on napkins, business cards, tablecloths and on my hand. Then I practised, practised, practised.

We're all public speakers. Whether it's on stage behind a microphone, in the pub with friends or over a dinner table. Others are impressed by your ability to recall jokes and tell them well.

A famous comedian once said to me "My ad-lib jokes aren't worth the paper they're written on."

Write them down. Categorise by punch line and practise on everyone. That's what I do. The highest paid people in the world are not those who know the most, it's those who are calculatingly funny. A good humorous T.V. host will be paid 10–20 times more than the head of the local university. We pay more for laughs than facts. We know that a speech which has humorous jokes, lines and cracks every 6–7 minutes is 200–400% more remembered than if the same speech is delivered without the humour. So it's a great way to teach facts. I've become so good at it that I've often been described as a cunning linguist.

HUMOUR HEALS
Norman Cousins was diagnosed with a terminal illness. The doctors told him that they could no longer help him and that he would soon die. So he checked into a hotel room and hired all the funny movies he could get and watched and re-watched them over and over, laughing as hard and loud as he could. After 6 months of this self-inflicted laughter therapy, the doctors were amazed to find that his illness had been completely cured – the cancer **gone**! This amazing result led to the publishing of the book *Anatomy of an Illness* by Norman Cousins and the start of massive research into the function of endorphins. Endorphin is a chemical substance that is released from the brain when you laugh. It has a similar chemical composition to morphine and heroin and has a tranquilising effect on the body while building the immune system. This explains why happy people rarely get sick and miserable and complaining people always seem to be ill.

Laughter and crying are closely linked from a psychological and physiological standpoint. Think of the last time someone told you a joke that made you buckle up with laughter. Where you couldn't control your laughing. How did you feel after? You felt a tingling sensation all over, right? Your brain released endorphins into your blood system that gave you what was once described as a "natural high"!! In effect, you were "stoned". Those who have trouble with laughing at life often turn to drugs and alcohol to achieve that same feeling. Alcohol loosens inhibitions and lets people laugh and release endorphins which is why most well-adjusted people laugh more when they drink alcohol and unhappy people become even more miserable or even violent.

At the end of a big laughing session, you will often cry. "I just laughed until I cried!" Tears have encaphlins which is another of the body's natural tranquillisers to relieve pain.

We cry when we experience a painful event and endorphins and encaphlins aid in self-anaesthesis.

The basis of many jokes is that something disastrous or painful happens to a person. But because we know that it is not a *real* event happening, we laugh and release endorphins for self-anaesthesis. If it *was* a real event, it is likely that we'd go immediately into crying mode and the body would also release encaphlins. This is why crying is often the extension of a laughing bout and why in a serious emotional crisis, such as a death, where many people cry, a person who cannot mentally accept the death may begin laughing. When the reality hits, the laughter turns to crying.

The bottom line? Laughter anaesthetises the body, builds the immune system, defends against illness and disease, teaches better and extends life. Humour heals.

THE LAUGHTER ROOM

In the 1980s several American hospitals introduced the concept of the "Laughter Room". Based on Norman Cousins' experiences, the room was filled with joke books, comedy films and humorous cassette tapes and had regular visits from comedians and clowns. The results? An improvement in patient health and shorter average hospitalisation time per patient.

The first Laughter Room was set up in Australia in 1995 at Moruya Hospital, New South Wales. Christine May from the South Coast Health Service said the Laughter Room was set up to improve the psychological and physiological well-being of the patients. "Research has now shown the positive effects of laughing such as the release of the body's own painkillers and improvement of the immune system. After laughter, the pulse rate steadies, breathing

11

deepens and the muscles relax. This all helps a patient get through an illness," she said. Executive In Charge of the Project, Margaret Thornton said "We have recorded shorter durations of stay for many patients, a decrease in the number of painkillers required by those in pain and patients are easier to deal with."

So I guess you could say they take their laughter seriously.

Humour Heals. He who laughs, lasts.

BEING OFFENDED

Political Correctness is a repressive system developed by university boffins, frustrated feminists and other unhappy people who have nothing better to do. As long as there are Irishmen, there will be Irish Jokes.

The English always tell Australian jokes about me. "You can tell an Australian – but you can't tell him much!" "What's the difference between Australia and yoghurt? At least yoghurt has some culture!" "Why are Aussies so well-balanced? They have a chip on both shoulders." "... and they're level-headed. They dribble out of both sides of their mouth."

As an Australian I don't choose to be offended. If it's a good joke (or true!) I'll laugh just as hard as the English. And later, I'll tell it against the Kiwis or the Yanks. Or write it in this book. Being offended is a choice. Others can't offend you – you **choose** to be offended. And choosing offence tells the world that you are unable to come to terms with the problems in your world.

So it doesn't make sense to choose offence. Or shame, embarrassment or feeling hurt. These choices show everyone that you have low self-esteem and aren't in control of your emotions. You can feel **offended** that it rains on your birthday party but the rain doesn't care – it just keeps raining.

You can choose to feel **embarrassed** because someone tells a joke that says your country persons are stupid. That doesn't mean that they *are* stupid and even if you agree that they are, abusing the joke-teller won't make them any smarter.

If you're a lawyer, you can choose to **feel hurt** because someone jokes that lawyers are liars. That doesn't mean that all lawyers are liars or that you are a liar. And reporting the joke-teller to the Thought Police won't stop him from thinking it. It only confirms that lawyers are worse than he thought!

You can choose **anger** because the traffic is backed up. But it won't clear the traffic. If you take a calm analytical approach about why the traffic is backed up you may come up with a solution that can help solve the problem. There's no point in choosing anger. Or telling the Thought Police about it.

Well, when I finished school my teacher Mr Spencer said it was a highlight for him to see the back of my head. And he told me so. He said I was a smartarse. I told him that a smartarse was anyone who could sit on an ice-cream and tell you what flavour it was. I guess he was right.

DON'T TAKE YOURSELF SERIOUSLY

Barbara Pease is my significant other (before Political Correctness she was my W.I.F.E. which means washing, ironing, fun and entertainment). She runs our company and travels the world. She doesn't, won't and isn't interested in cooking. Where other husbands will get pot roast, I'll get roast pot. If she cooks, we all pray before we eat, even though we're not religious. She gave my penis a name – Willy. She says all men should name their penises because you don't want a complete stranger to make all your major life decisions. Whenever she sees me she smiles – which proves she can recognise a joke. She told me that I was ready for marriage when I met her because I wore an earring. I'd experienced pain and bought jewellery.

The best humour you can tell is on *yourself*.

Take what you do seriously. But never take yourself seriously.

A WORD ON DISCRIMINATION

There's a paradox here – if you insult or offend **one** person or **one** group you can be accused of being discriminatory. If you offend **everyone** you won't be accused.

This book is definitely non-discriminatory. **Everyone** gets a serve.

Allan Pease

CONTENTS

LAWYERS AND JUDGES

The lawyer went into the doctor's surgery with a frog on his head.

"That's a nasty looking growth," said the doctor.

"I'll say it is," said the frog. "It started out as a pimple on my arse."

***

What's the difference between a prostitute and a lawyer?

Not much, except a prostitute will stop screwing you once you're dead.

***

What's black and brown and looks great on a lawyer?
A Doberman.

***

"I'm in deep financial trouble and need some advice," said the client to his lawyer. "I'm down to my last hundred dollars and want to know if you can answer just two questions for that amount."

"Certainly sir," said the lawyer, "what's the second question?"

***

A new law says that solicitors and barristers must be buried in holes forty feet deep.

Deep down, they are good people.

***

"**Y**ou seem like an intelligent, honest man who wouldn't lie to the court," the lawyer said sarcastically to the witness.

"If I wasn't under oath I'd return the compliment," said the witness.

***

The clerk addressed the prisoner in the dock. "Prisoner, do you wish to challenge the jury?"

The prisoner looked at the jury. "Not all of them at once," he said, "but I reckon I could go a few rounds with the little fat guy in the middle."

***

What's the difference between a lawyer and a football?

You only get six points for kicking a football between the posts.

***

What is it that a lawyer can do that a duck can't?

Stick his bill up his arse.

***

What's the difference between a catfish and a lawyer?

One's a bottom-crawling scum sucker, and the other's a fish.

***

Did you hear about the lawyer who was so big that when he died they couldn't find a coffin big enough to hold the body.

They gave him an enema and buried him in a hat box.

***

Obscenity is anything that gives the Judge a hard-on.

***

What do you call a barrister with an I.Q. of 25?
Your Honour.

***

"Do you know how to save a lawyer from drowning?"
"No, I don't."
"Good!"

***

He introduced himself as a criminal lawyer.

"Well, at least you're honest about describing yourself," said the client.

***

The university has stopped using rats for experiments. They've decided to use lawyers for three reasons.

1. Lawyers are more plentiful than rats.
2. Some rats are nice and you can get attached to them.
3. There are some things that rats just won't do.

But they had to stop using lawyers and they're back to using rats, because they found that lawyers aren't that close to human beings.

***

What's 12 inches long, transparent and lies in the gutter?

A lawyer with the shit kicked out of him.

***

The young lawyer had just opened for business. He had been sitting behind his desk for a week when at last he saw a man come into his outer office. Quickly he picked up the phone and pretended to be negotiating a big deal. He spoke loudly about large sums of money and possible Court proceedings. When he hung up, he looked at the visitor and asked, "Can I help you?"

"Yes," said the man, "I've come to connect your phone."

***

Why don't you ever see lawyers at the beach?

The cats keep covering them up with sand.

***

Two lawyers were walking along, negotiating a case.

"Look," said one to the other, "let's be honest with each other."

"Okay, you first," replied the other.

That was the end of the discussion.

***

What do lawyers use for birth control?
Their personalities.

***

A lawyer was visiting Bangkok. He went to the most exclusive Escort Agency and asked if he could take Sue-Lin to dinner.

"Yes," said the Madam. "It will cost you $300 for Sue-Lin's company. No sex. And she must be back here at 11 p.m."

Sue-Lin was the most beautiful Eurasian creature the lawyer had ever seen. He wined her and dined her, but before returning her home, he gave her $1,000. "This is a gift," he said.

Sue-Lin told him that he was a wonderful and generous man.

"Will you have dinner with me again tomorrow night?" he asked.

"Oh yes," she replied. "I will cancel all my previous arrangements."

So the next night, the lawyer wined and dined Sue-Lin again. He could not get over her beauty, and at the end of the evening, gave her another $1,000 and said, "Sue-Lin, this is for you."

Sue-Lin was overcome with gratitude and had a tear in her eye. "You are the most generous person I have ever met," she said.

"Would you come to dinner with me again tomorrow night?" asked the lawyer.

"Of course I will!" said Sue-Lin. "I will do anything for such a kind, generous man."

So he wined and dined Sue-Lin again, and took her back to her apartment, where he gave her another $1,000. This overwhelmed Sue-Lin. She fell into the lawyer's arms and then onto the bed, where they made passionate love until three in the morning. The lawyer told Sue-Lin that he had to leave as he was catching a plane for Sydney at six o'clock that morning.

"Sydney!" said Sue-Lin. "You didn't tell me you came from Sydney! I have a sister who lives in Sydney!"

"Yes, I know," said the lawyer. "She sent you the $3,000."

***

When Pope John Paul died, he arrived at the Pearly Gates at the same time as a lawyer. Both were ushered in to see St. Peter. He gave the lawyer a mansion with a swimming pool and the Pope had to share a double room and an old T.V. set. The Pope was disappointed and queried this decision. St. Peter explained.

"We've got a hundred Popes up here, but that's the first lawyer."

***

What do you call a bigot with a wig?
Your Honour.

***

"On what grounds do you want a divorce?" asked the lawyer.

"Cruelty," she replied. "Every night he wants sex and his donk is as big as a horse. It hurts unbearably."

"If that's the case, I will file your petition," said the. lawyer.

"File my petition? Not likely! Let the bastard sandpaper his."

***

It was a sexual harassment case, and it had been a long day. The young lady accusing her boss said that she was too embarrassed to repeat the words that he said to her. The judge suggested she write them down and that the words be shown to himself and the jury.

She passed the note, which read "Get your pants off and have a drink with me tonight", to the judge, who then passed it on to Fred, the foreperson of the jury. Fred passed it on to the next juror, a middle-aged spinster who had nodded off in the stuffy courtroom. He had to nudge her. She woke, read the note, winked at Fred and put the note in her handbag,

***

"Have you anything to say for yourself?" asked the judge after hearing the case.

"Fuck all," muttered the defendant.

"What did he say?" asked the judge, who was a bit hard of hearing.

The clerk whispered in the judge's ear. "He said 'Fuck all', Your Worship."

"That's funny," said the judge, "I'm sure I saw his lips move."

RELIGION

Sister Mary and Sister Barbara were driving along a country road when the Devil appeared on the bonnet of their car and made menacing gestures.

"Quick," said Sister Mary, "show him your cross!"

Sister Barbara leaned out the window and yelled, "Piss off, you bastard! I'll kick you in the balls if you try that again! Don't mess with me, you prick!"

***

The Pope's doctor had told him that his celibacy was causing serious health problems. The doctor recommended that the Pope have regular sex with a woman or else he could die. The Pope resisted this suggestion for some time, but finally came to realise that it was the only answer.

"OK, I'll do it," he said, "but on three conditions. First she must be Catholic, second she must live in the local parish, and third it must be completely confidential."

As the doctor was leaving the room the Pope yelled, "... and by the way Doc, can you get me one with big tits?"

***

The Evangelist settled into his motel room after a busy day of rousing, table-thumping delivery of his message to the public. Before heading downstairs for a nightcap, he flipped idly through the Gideon Bible which sat on his bedside table, as indeed it does in every motel room throughout the world.

Downstairs in the bar he soon formed a chatty association with the barmaid, and, with his usual gift of the gab, invited her to his room for a blessing. A few more drinks and hands-on healing and it wasn't long before they were getting into a very ticklish situation.

"Are you sure this is all right," giggled the barmaid. "You are a man of the cloth."

He reassured her, "It is permissible, my child. It is written in the Bible," after which he proceeded to have his way with her.

Whilst enjoying a post-coital cigarette, the barmaid turned to him and said, "Show me – where is it written in the Bible that it was all right to do what we did?"

Whereupon he picked up the Bible, turned to the inside cover and showed her the passage written there: "The downstairs barmaid is a certainty."

***

Why was Jesus crucified and not electrocuted?

Because if they had electrocuted him, today, 100 million Catholics wouldn't bless themselves with a cross. They would scream "Aaaarrrrgggghhh!" and shake.

**

As the shop steward passed his local church, the large sign proclaimed, **"Jesus Lives!"** Hurrying to the Union office, he worriedly queried, "Does this mean no more Easter holidays?"

**

The crowd had gathered around Mary Magdalene, preparing to stone her. Jesus held up his hand and said, "Whoever is without sin, let them cast the first stone."

Out of the crowd came a rock. It hit Mary Magdalene on the head and killed her. Jesus looked exasperated and yelled, "Mother, sometimes you just piss me off."

**

Sitting in the plane was a bishop and a young priest. The bishop was doing *The Times* crossword.

"Four letter word, exclusively female, ends in UNT," he mumbled.

"Aunt," suggested the young priest.

"Oh," said the bishop, "have you got an eraser?"

**

The white missionary was in big trouble. The tribal chief was very angry.

"My sister had a white baby last night and you're the only white man in this area. You must die for this breach of tribal law."

"But Chief!" said the missionary nervously, "I know it looks that way but these things happen. For instance, see your flock of sheep over there? Can you see the black sheep? There is only one."

"All right, all right," replied the Chief, "I'll keep quiet if you'll keep quiet."

***

O'Brien was dying.

"Sister," he said, "call the vicar."

"Don't you want a priest?"

"No, I want to become a Protestant," said O'Brien. "Better one of those bastards die instead of a good Catholic."

***

Pat and Mick were working on the road outside the local whorehouse when they saw the vicar approach, look cautiously around and enter the building.

"Look at that!" said Pat. "That dirty Protestant minister! What a hypocrite!"

Not long after, they noticed a rabbi approach, look cautiously around and enter the building.

"Did you see that?" said Mick. "The bloody Jews are no better."

Half an hour went by, when they noticed Father O'Flanagan looking furtively about before dashing in to the whorehouse.

"Mick," said Pat, "take off your hat. One of those poor girls must be dying in there."

***

The young man entered the confessional box.

"Father, I had sex with a pair of beautiful eighteen-year-old nymphomaniac twins every night last week."

"Disgusting! What kind of Catholic are you?" reproached the priest.

"I'm not a Catholic," he replied.

"Then why are you telling me this?"

"I'm telling everyone!"

***

Pat and Mick went into Dublin every Saturday night together. Pat always went to confession at the local church on the way while Mick waited outside.

"It's been a week since my last confession, Father," said Pat, "and I must confess that I have sinned of the flesh again."

"Was it Mary Fitzgerald, that hussy from the dairy?"

"No, Father."

"Was it Maureen O'Connor from the fruit shop then?"

"No, Father."

"Then it must have been Kathleen Dwyer."

"No, Father."

"Well, do your usual fifty Hail Marys and thirty-five Our Fathers and be off with you."

Pat joined Mick outside the church and Mick asked, "What did you get?"

"I got three certainties for tonight!" replied Pat.

***

Mary was entering the church. She had no head covering and was wearing a see-through blouse.

"You can't come into church like that!" exclaimed the priest.

"But I have a divine right!" replied Mary.

"You have a divine left too, but you still can't come in without a hat."

***

"What's this?" (hold your palm up to your mouth and make biting gestures)

Jesus biting his nails.

***

The Hindu rushed into St Patrick's Cathedral and cried, "My Karma has just run over your Dogma."

***

Adam was the world's first butcher.

He was always chasing Eve with his meat waggin'.

***

The drunk boarded the bus, took a seat next to a priest and began reading his newspaper. After a while, in a slurred voice, the drunk asked the priest, "Do you know what causes arthritis?"

The priest looked at the drunk disdainfully. "Yes, my man. I can tell you. It's too much alcohol! Too much immoral living! Too much smoking. How long have you had it?"

"S'not me," said the drunk. "It sez here the Pope's got it."

***

Eve was the first carpenter.

She made Adam's banana stand.

***

What's the difference between a Catholic priest and a pimple?

Nothing – they both come on a boy's face when he turns thirteen.

***

What's white and drips from clouds?

The coming of the Lord.

***

The Sunday School teacher asked the class, "Who went to Mount Olive?"

"Popeye!" came the quick reply.

***

The proud father handed the baby to the priest for the christening.

"And what name have you given this little boy?" asked the priest.

"It's a girl," said the father out of the side of his mouth "You've got hold of my thumb."

***

What's the difference between a woman in church and a woman in the bath?

One has a soul full of hope.

***

They were a very religious couple. They had attended church and prayed together for many years, and this was their wedding night. He changed into his pyjamas in the bathroom and when he came back into the bedroom, his bride was naked between the sheets.

"I thought I would find you on your knees," he said.

"Oh, we can do it that way too, but I thought tonight I'd like to see your face," she replied.

JOKES ABOUT WOMEN

Because We Are Men

If we put a woman on a pedestal and try to protect her from the Rat Race, we're a male chauvinist pig. If we stay at home and do the housework, we're a pansy. If we work too hard, there is never any time for her and the kids. If we don't work hard enough, we're a good for nothing layabout. If she has a boring repetitive job with low pay, that is exploitation. If we have a boring repetitive job with low pay, we should get off our butts and find something better.

If a man gets a promotion ahead of her, that is favouritism. If she gets a promotion ahead of a man, that is equal opportunity.

If we mention how nice she looks, that is sexual harassment. If we keep quiet, that is typical male indifference. If we cry, we're a wimp. If we don't, we're an insensitive bastard.

If a man thumps her, that is wife bashing. If she thumps him, that's self-defence.

If he makes a decision without consulting her, he's a chauvinist. If she makes a decision without regard for his feelings, then she's a liberated woman. If he asks her to do something she doesn't enjoy, that is domination. If she asks him it's a favour.

If we appreciate the female form and frilly underwear we're sexual perverts. If we don't notice, we're poofters. If we like a woman to keep in shape and shave her legs, that is sexist. If we don't care, that is unromantic. If we try to keep ourselves in shape, that is vanity. If we don't, we're slobs.

If we buy her flowers, we're after something. If we don't, we're forgetful. If we are proud of our achievements, we're full of ourselves. If we aren't, we're not ambitious. If we ask for a cuddle, we never think of anything else but sex. If we're totally wrecked after a bad day at the office, we never give a stuff about other people's needs.

If she has a headache, it's because she's tired. If he has a headache, it's because he doesn't love her anymore. If we want sex too often, we're oversexed. If we can't perform on cue, there must be someone else.

***

Why are pubic hairs curly?
  So they don't poke you in the eye.

***

I can't get over a girl like you ... so answer the phone yourself.

***

What's the difference between a woman with her period and a terrorist?
  You can negotiate with a terrorist.

***

What's the definition of "making love"?
It's what a woman does while a man's screwing her.

***

A woman's best friends are her legs, but even best friends must part.

***

Man cannot live on bread alone. He must have a bit of crumpet.

***

Why does it take a woman with P.M.S. three hours to cook a small chicken?
BECAUSE IT JUST FUCKIN' DOES!!!!!!!

***

What's the difference between a woman and a washing machine?
A washing machine doesn't ring you up constantly after you've left a load in it.

***

Jenny Jones woke up one night to find her husband pushing aspirin into her mouth.
"What do you think you're doing?" she screamed at him.
"It's for your headache," he replied.
"I haven't got a headache," she gasped.
"Great! Let's fuck!"

Have you heard about the latest bra for middle-aged women?

It's called Sheep Dog. It rounds them up and points them in the right direction.

***

Why was alcohol invented?

So ugly women could get laid too.

DOGS ARE BETTER THAN WOMEN BECAUSE ......

- Dogs don't cry
- Dogs love it when your friends come over
- Dogs don't care if you use their shampoo
- Dogs think you're a great singer
- Dogs don't expect you to call when you run late
- The later you are, the more excited dogs are to see you
- Dogs will forgive you for playing around with other dogs
- Dogs don't notice if you call them by another dog's name
- Dogs are excited by rough play
- Dogs don't mind if you give their offspring away
- Dogs understand that farts are funny
- Dogs can appreciate excessive body hair
- Dogs like it when you leave things on the floor
- A dog's disposition stays the same all month long
- Dogs never need to examine the relationship
- Dogs' parents never visit
- Dogs love long car trips
- Dogs understand that instincts are better than asking for directions
- Dogs never criticise

- Dogs agree that you have to raise your voice to get your point across
- Dogs never expect gifts
- Dogs don't worry about germs
- Dogs don't want to know about every other dog you've ever had
- Dogs don't let magazine articles guide their lives
- Dogs would rather you buy them a hamburger dinner than a lobster one
- Dogs don't keep you waiting
- Dogs enjoy heavy petting in public
- Dogs find you amusing when you're drunk

***

A man and a woman were in an elevator in the Empire State Building when the cable broke. As the elevator plummeted down, the woman looked at the man and said, "Is there one more chance of being a woman?"

"There sure is," said the man as he quickly pulled his trousers off. He threw them at her, saying, "Here, iron these!"

THE LAST 10 THINGS A WOMAN WOULD EVER SAY

1   Could our relationship be more physical? I'm tired of just being friends.

2   Go ahead and leave the seat up. I love the feel of cold, wet porcelain.

3   I think hairy bums are really sexy.

4   Wow, get a whiff of that one! Do it again.

5   Please don't throw that old t-shirt away. The holes in the armpits are just too cute.

6   This diamond is much too big!

7   I won't even put my lips on that thing unless I get to swallow!

8   Wow, it really is ten inches!

9   Does this make my bum look too small?

10 I'm wrong. You must be right again.

***

What do women and cow-pats have in common?
The older they get, the easier they are to pick up.

***

The woman of the 90s is well educated, well dressed, highly motivated, professionally oriented, drives a B.M.W. and thinks that cooking and fucking are cities in China.

***

Women have only got themselves to blame for all the lying that men do.
They ask too many questions.

***

They've just released a new Barbie Doll called Divorced Barbie.
It comes with all Ken's stuff.

***

JOKES ABOUT MEN

The Rules According to a Woman

1   The woman always makes the Rules.

2   The Rules are subject to change at any time without prior notification.

3   No man can possibly know all the Rules.

4   If the woman suspects the man knows the Rules, she must immediately change some or all of the Rules.

5   The woman is never wrong.

6   If the woman is wrong, it is due to misunderstanding, which was a direct result of something the man did or said.

7   The man must apologise immediately for causing said misunderstanding.

8   The woman may change her mind at any time.

9   The man must never change his mind without the express written consent of the woman.

10   The woman has every right to be angry and/or upset at any time.

11   The man must remain calm at all times unless the woman wants him to be angry and/or upset.

12   The woman must, under no circumstances, let the man know whether or not she wants him to be angry and/or upset.

13   The man is expected to mind-read at all times.

14 The man who doesn't abide by the Rules can't take the heat, lacks backbone and is a wimp.

15 Any attempt to document the Rules could result in bodily harm.

16 If the woman has PMT, all the Rules are null and void.

17 The woman is ready when she is ready.

18 The man must be ready at all times.

***

Adam came first. But men always do.

***

What's the difference between a '90s woman and a computer?

A '90s woman won't accept a three-and-a-half-inch floppy.

***

"Of course there's nobody else!" she said to her doubting boyfriend. "Do you think I'd be going out with a dickhead like you if there was?"

***

What's the difference between a new husband and a new dog?

After twelve months the dog is still excited to see you.

***

What is a major conflict of interest for men?
When pizza arrives during sex.

***

How do men practise safe sex?
They meet their mistress at least 30 kilometres from where they live.

***

What can you say to a man who's just had sex?
Anything you like – he's asleep.

***

Why do men find it difficult to make eye contact?
Breasts don't have eyes.

***

"God, why did you make woman so beautiful?" he asked.
"So you would love her," God replied.
"But God, why did you make her so dumb?" he asked.
"So she would love you."

***

The feminists were all hailing the Miracle Birth – the baby had both a dick and a brain.

***

Bob was going over the household budget and was complaining to his wife about her expenditure.

"You can clean the house yourself," he said. "That will save on the cleaning lady.

"You can also learn to cook. That will save on restaurants.

"And while you're at it, you should learn to iron, so we won't have to pay the ironing lady."

"And you should learn to fuck," said his wife, "then we could get rid of the gardener."

***

When a woman marries she expects three S's: sensitivity, sincerity and sharing. What does she get? The three B's: burps, body odour and beer breath.

***

What's a man's idea of helping to make the bed?
He gets out of it.

***

Marriage is the price men pay for sex and sex is the price women pay for marriage.

***

Why are men like public toilets?
They're either vacant, engaged or full of shit.

***

20 Reasons Why Women Prefer Chocolate to Sex:

1 You can get plenty of chocolate.
2 Chocolate satisfies you even when it goes soft.
3 You can safely have chocolate while you're driving.
4 You can make chocolate last as long as you want it to.
5 You can have chocolate anywhere (even in front of your mother).
6 If you bite the nuts too hard, chocolate won't mind.
7 Two women can have chocolate together and not be called dykes.
8 You can ask a stranger for chocolate and not get a bad reputation.
9 You won't get hair in your mouth when you suck on chocolate.
10 "If you love me, you'll swallow it" has real meaning with chocolate.
11 With chocolate there's no need to fake enjoyment.
12 Chocolate doesn't make you pregnant.
13 You can have chocolate at any time of the month.
14 You're never too old for chocolate.
15 When you're having chocolate, it doesn't keep anyone awake in the next room.
16 Even small chocolates are good.
17 You can have chocolate with kids and not go to jail.
18 Chocolate doesn't keep you awake snoring after you've had it.
19 You can have chocolate all weekend and still walk OK on Monday.
20 It's easy to find eight inches of chocolate.

***

He was very suave and as he slid up to a blonde at the singles bar, he thought he'd try out his new pick-up line.

"Hi beautiful. I'd love to get into your pants."

"Why?" she replied. "There's already one arsehole in there."

***

The elderly spinster was asked why she never married.

"I have a dog that growls, a parrot that swears, a fire-place that smokes and a cat that stays out all night. Why would I want a husband?"

***

I believe in circumcision – it's no skin off my nose.

***

THE LAST TEN THINGS MEN WOULD EVER SAY

10 I think Barry Manilow is really cool.

9 While I'm up, can I get you a cup of coffee?

8 I think hairy legs are really sexy.

7 Her tits are just too big.

6 Sometimes I just want to be held.

5 That chick on *Murder, She Wrote* gives me a hard-on.

4 Sure, I'd love to wear a condom.

3 We haven't been dress shopping for ages. Let's go now. Can I carry your purse for you?

2 Fuck Monday night footy. Let's watch *Ready, Steady, Cook*.

1 I think we're lost. I'll pull over and ask for directions.

***

What's the definition of the perfect male lover?
He makes love until 2 a.m. then turns into chocolate.

***

Why do most men prefer women with big tits and tight twats?
Because most men have big mouths and small dicks.

***

Why do men cum quickly?
So they can rush down to the pub and tell their mates.

***

The marriage counsellor asked her why she felt the relationship was over.
"Because he's a lousy lover," she replied.
The counsellor asked the husband how he felt about it.
He replied, "How can she tell that in three minutes?"

***

"Darling," he said, "am I the first man to make love to you?"
"Well you could be ... were you behind the stage of the Rolling Stones concert in 1973?"

***

"Darling, am I the first man to make love to you?"
"You could be ... you look kinda familiar."

***

I went to the doctor about my piles and he told me I had beautiful firm breasts, just like an eighteen-year-old."

"Oh yes?" smirked her husband. "But what did he say about your forty-five-year-old arse?"

"Your name wasn't mentioned," she replied.

FEMINISTS ON MEN

Why does a woman need an arsehole?
Someone's got to put out the garbage.

***

How many men does it take to change a light bulb?
Ten. One to change the bulb and nine to pin the medal on his chest.

***

Why do men have holes in the end of their penises?
To get air to their brains.

***

When a woman makes a fool of a man, it's usually an improvement.

***

Men prefer looks to brains because most men see better than they think.

***

A woman only wants to have a child, not marry one.

***

Some women get excited about nothing, then marry him.

***

Why is a pig better than a man?
  Pigs don't turn into men when they have too much to drink.

***

Women can take a joke – they get married to prove it!

***

What do you call a man who has lost 99% of his brains?
  A widower.

***

When you look at the worms we pick up, it's no wonder men call us Birds.

***

What is the useless bit of skin at the end of a penis called?
  A man.

***

"Doctor, I have a small embarrassing wart."
"Then divorce him."

***

Modern women think of having children at age 35.
At age 35, modern men think of dating children.

***

Why did Dorothy get lost in the Land of Oz?
Because she had three men giving her directions.

***

What's the difference between a man with a mid-life crisis and a circus clown?
A circus clown knows he's wearing funny clothes.

***

What's the best way of making sure your man doesn't make a fool of himself at a party?
Leave him at home.

***

What can you immediately tell about the guys down the gym who parade around showing off their perfect bodies?
They're unemployed.

***

Why is it a waste of time telling a man to go to hell?
He'd get lost on the way.

***

What do men and pantyhose have in common?
They cling to women but one rough spot and watch them run!

***

How can you be sure a man is planning for the future?
He buys two cases of beer instead of one.

***

How are men like bread?
They're easier to take when you butter them up.

***

Why are men like babies?
They make a fuss when you try to change them.

***

Why are men like vending machines?
They'll take your money and half the time they won't work.

***

What's a man's idea of helping out around the house?
He drops his clothes where it's easy for you to pick them up.

***

What recycling do most men do?
They use their beer cans as ashtrays before throwing them on the side of the road.

***

Why did Moses spend 40 years wandering in the desert?
He refused to ask for directions.

***

Why are bachelors like used cars?
They're easy to find, cheap and unreliable.

***

What's the difference between a clitoris and a hotel bar?
Most men can find a bar in under four minutes.

***

Any woman who thinks that the way to a man's heart is through his stomach is aiming too high.

***

What do men and floor tiles have in common?
If you lay them properly, you can walk over them forever.

***

She was looking for a husband so she put an ad in the Lonely Hearts column. She got fifty replies, all saying "You can have mine."

***

Why do men always have a stupid look on their face?
Because they are stupid.

***

"My boyfriend's a SNAG," said Jody. "A Sensitive New Age Guy."
"That's nice," replied Carol. "Mine's a Caring Understanding Nineties Type."

***

Any woman who strives to be equal to a man has a poor self image.

***

What is the thinnest book in the world?
Everything Men Know About Women.

***

How can you tell if a man is sexually excited?
He's breathing.

***

Why are blonde jokes so short?
So men can remember them.

***

What is a man's idea of foreplay?
Half an hour of begging.

***

How can you tell if a man is happy?
Who cares?

***

Why are men and parking spots similar?
The good ones are already taken and the ones that are left are handicapped.

***

What do men and beer bottles have in common?
They're both empty from the neck up.

***

How many men does it take to screw in a light bulb?
One. Men will screw anything.

***

Why do women rub their eyes when they wake up?
Because they don't have balls to scratch.

***

Why don't men have to use toilet paper?
Because God made them perfect arseholes.

***

How do you save a man from drowning?
Take your foot off his head.

***

What do you call a man with an I.Q. of 50?
Gifted.

***

How many men does it take to change a roll of toilet paper?
It's unknown 'cos it's never happened.

***

What do toilet seats, anniversaries and a clitoris have in common?
Men miss them all.

***

How do you keep a man interested after marriage?
Wear perfume that smells like beer.

***

Why do men marry women who remind them of their mothers?

Who else would put up with them?

***

Colleen had just accepted Paddy's proposal of marriage and had asked him home for the weekend to meet her parents. Innocently she burst into the bathroom and saw Paddy standing naked. She ran to her mother and asked, "Mother, what's that thing hanging between Paddy's legs?"

"Don't worry, that's his penis, it's nothing to be concerned about."

"But what's that big purple knob on the end?" asked Colleen.

"That's just the head," her mother replied.

"And what are those two round things about 18 inches back from the head?" asked Colleen.

"Well," said the mother, "for your sake, I hope they're the cheeks of his arse."

***

The annoyed wife phoned her husband at the club, told him how late it was and politely suggested he should come home. Now.

"But darling," the man pleaded, "I'm playing the slot machines. I can't quit now. I'm on a winning streak. I've got a stack of 20 pence pieces as long as my dick."

"Huh!" snorted his wife. "You mean to tell me all you've got left is a lousy two quid?"

***

What is the difference between medium and rare?

Six inches is medium, eight inches is rare.

***

CATHOLICS

"I'd like a bottle of Johnny Walker please," Sister Mary asked the surprised bartender. "It's OK ... It's for Mother Superior's constipation."

Later that day the licensee was shocked to see the nun sitting in the park, pissed.

"Didn't you say that whiskey was for Mother Superior's constipation?" he asked.

"It is," slurred Sister Mary, "... and when she sees me she'll shit."

***

The old nun was lecturing the drinker on the evils of drink as he tried to enter the pub.

"Listen Sister," he said, "don't knock it if you've never tried it! If you'd tried even one drink you'd know what you are talking about."

She agreed that he had a point.

"OK, I'll try just a small drink then," she said. "I don't want to be seen drinking from a hotel glass so can you get me some in this water flask?"

He went up to the bar and asked for a gin in the flask.

The barman laughed, "Don't tell me that damn nun's still out there!"

***

The priest found a quiet corner for his usual morning fondle and got so carried away he didn't see the tourist looking through the window and the flash of a camera told him he'd been sprung. He chased the tourist and begged, "I'll buy the film."

"No, you'll buy the camera!" said the tourist smugly.

"How much?"

"$3,000."

"That's robbery!" said the indignant priest. But he had little choice so he paid it. Later, Sister Beatrice noticed the priest's new camera.

"How much did you pay for that?" she asked.

"$3,000!"

"My God," she said. "Somebody must have seen you coming!"

***

Two nuns are cycling down a cobblestone street. The first one says to the other, "I haven't come this way before."

The second replies, "Me neither. Must be the cobbles."

***

How do you get a nun pregnant?

Dress her up as an altar boy.

***

Father Ryan was giving the nuns their last bit of advice before they set forth into the wide world from their Convent.

"There will be many a wicked man trying to take sexual liberties with you," he said, "but always remember that one hour of pleasure could ruin the whole of your careers. Has anyone got any questions?"

"Yes, Father. How do you make it last an hour?"

***

Zoos are a place for the most unusual accidents. One day, Sister Mary leant too close to the gorillas' cage. The big silverback reached out and grabbed her, pulled her through the bars, tore off her habit and screwed her.

When she was finally rescued, she was admitted to the hospital in a state of shock. It was a week before Mother Superior could speak to her. Sister Mary was crying uncontrollably.

"What's wrong?" asked the Mother Superior. "Why are you still so upset?"

"How would you feel?" sobbed Sister Mary. "It's been a week and he hasn't written, hasn't phoned."

***

Christian Brothers are dedicated to the education of children. One Brother and a lay-teacher were taking a class of children on a holiday. They were travelling by plane. The pilot rushed into the cabin and shouted, "We're out of fuel. The plane is going to crash. There are only two parachutes on board. I've got one. You must decide who is going to have the other one."

The Christian Brothers said, "We can strap two children together in the one parachute."

The lay-teacher said, "Fuck the children."

The Christian Brother replied, "Do you think we've got time?"

***

Six-year-old Susie comes home and announces, "Mum, God's got a name."

"Really!" said the mother. "How do you know that?"

"In school today, they taught us that God's name is Harold."

"Harold?" replied the mother. "Why Harold?"

"Well" replied the six-year-old, "they taught me this poem –

Our Father, who are in Heaven
Harold be thy name ...."

There was an earthquake and the Christian Brothers Monastery was levelled. All fifty Brothers were transported to Heaven at the one time.

At the Pearly Gates, St. Peter said, "Let's go through the entry test as a group. Now, first question. How many of you have played around with little boys?"

Forty-nine hands went up.

"Right!" said St. Peter. "You forty-nine can go down to Purgatory and take that deaf bastard with you!"

MAGIC LAMPS

A drunk walked into the bar carrying a small case. He put the case on the bar and said to the barman, "I bet you a double scotch I can show you the most amazing thing you've ever seen."

"I've seen some pretty amazing things," said the barman, "but I accept the bet."

The drunk opened his case and there was a pianist 12 inches tall, sitting down playing a piano.

"I've never seen anything like it!" said the barman. "Where did you get that?"

"Well," said the drunk, "I dug up this old lamp and when I rubbed it a genie appeared and said I could have one wish."

"What did you ask for?"

"A 12-inch penis!" said the drunk.

***

"Could I rub the lantern?" said the barman.

"Certainly," said the drunk.

The barman rubbed the lamp and a genie appeared.

"What is your one wish?" said the genie.

"I wish I had a million bucks," said the barman, and instantly the bar was full of ducks – a million of them.

"I forgot to tell you," said the drunk, "the genie's got very poor hearing."

***

A man is walking along a deserted beach and finds a bottle and rubs it. A genie appears and grants him any wish.

"I wish I was always hard, and could get more arse than anybody."

So the genie turned him into a seat in a public toilet.

***

Ray was on holiday in Bangkok when he visited an antiques shop and spotted a little ivory idol in the corner of the shop. As he studied it closely he was surprised when it spoke to him.

"Please help me kind Sir. I'm not really an ivory idol, I'm a beautiful young princess, trapped in here by a wicked witch's spell. I need someone to have sex with me to break the spell."

"I'll talk to my brother-in-law about it," said Ray, "he's an idle fucking bastard."

***

John sat still as the fortune-teller gazed into her crystal ball. Suddenly, she started to laugh uncontrollably so John leaned across and punched her in the nose.

It was the first time he had struck a happy medium.

***

Three men are walking down the beach when they find an old lantern in the sand. One gives it a rub and a genie appears. The genie says, "You can have one wish each."

The first guy thinks for a few minutes and says, "I would like to be a hundred times smarter than I am now."

"Your wish is granted," says the genie.

The second guy blurts out, "I'd like to be a thousand times smarter than I am now."

"Your wish is granted," says the genie.

The third guy thinks hard and long and decides, "I would like to be ten thousand times smarter than I am now."

The genie grants his wish, and he turns into a woman.

***

A man is walking on a beach when a bottle washes up on the shore. He opens it and a genie appears and grants him any one wish.

But he's a little embarrassed about his wish, so he whispers it in the genie's ear.

"Tonight at midnight," says the genie, "your front doorbell will ring and your wish will be granted." He rushes home and waits excitedly. As the clock chimes twelve, the doorbell rings. He opens the door and sees 3 jockeys standing there wearing white hoods and holding a noose.

"Are you the guy who wants to be hung like a donkey?" they ask.

***

The tourist was visiting a Greek fishing village and noticed that a local fisherman had a head no bigger than a tennis ball.

"Why is your head so small?" asked the tourist.

"Well," said the fisherman, "many years ago, I caught a mermaid in my nets. I was going to sell her to a marine park when she said, 'Let me free and I will grant you three wishes.'"

"I would like a beautiful new fishing boat," he said, and lo and behold, a lovely big trawler appeared.

"I wish to be wealthy," he added, and instantly the deck of his new boat was covered with gold ingots.

The fisherman thought how beautiful the mermaid was and said, "For my third and last wish, I wish to make love to you."

"But you can't," replied the mermaid. "I am only half woman."

"Well," said the fisherman, "how about giving me a little head?"

***

Harry was shipwrecked on a tropical island for twelve months. One day out of the surf came a stunning blonde dressed in scuba gear. Slowly, languidly, voluptuously, she walked down the beach and laid down beside Harry.

"Would you like a cigarette?" she purred in his ear.

"Are you kidding!" said Harry.

She unzipped a pocket of her wetsuit, pulled out a packet of cigarettes, lit one for Harry and put it in his mouth.

Then she asked, "How about a nice cold beer?"

"Yes! Yes! Yes!" cried Harry.

She unzipped another pocket, produced two glasses and a bottle and poured them both a drink.

She moved closer to him, whispering seductively in his ear, "How would you like to play around?"

"Oh God!" said Harry disbelievingly, "don't tell me you've got golf clubs in there too!"

***

ACCOUNTANTS

What do you call ten accountants buried up to their necks in sand?

Soccer practice.

ACUMEN

Doctor Watson was told by Sherlock Holmes' gardener that a schoolgirl was in Holmes' bedroom. Watson heard muffled sounds coming from the bedroom and, fearing that Holmes was in danger, broke down the door to find Holmes and the girl having a 69.

"Holmes!" said Watson. "What kind of a schoolgirl is this?"

"Elementary, my dear Watson, Elementary."

***

Two young men were in court on charges of heroin trafficking. Before sentencing, the judge said, "We have just designed a rehabilitation program, and if you two are prepared to become involved, I will consider not ordering a jail sentence. What I want you to do is spend a hundred hours of your own time trying to reform drug addicts. Do you accept this challenge?"

Both men accepted. "Further," said the judge, "I want you to report back to me on a monthly basis."

At the end of the first month, the first man claimed that he had influenced thirty-five men to enter into a rehabilitation program.

"Remarkable!" said the judge. "How did you accomplish that?"

"Well," replied the first man, "I draw two circles – a large circle, which I mark 'A' and a small circle inside the large circle which I call 'B'. I explain to the drug addicts that before they start taking dope, their brain is as large as 'A' but after they've been on dope for a couple of years or so, it finishes up the size of 'B', which means you finish up a moron. Then you'll go to jail. This seems to have the required impact and they consent to go onto a rehabilitation program."

"Excellent!" said the judge excitedly. "Now, how did you go?" he said to the second man.

"Well, I got nine hundred men to enter the rehabilitation program, using the same method but a different story."

"That's amazing! How?" enquired the judge.

"I draw a large circle 4 inches in diameter, and mark it 'A', and put a small circle in the centre which is about one inch in diameter and mark it 'B', and I tell them that after they've been on dope for a few years, they'll get caught and go to jail. Before they go to jail, their arsehole will be as big as circle 'B', and after they've been in jail for three months, it'll be as big as circle 'A', and this seems to have the desired effect."

**

He was an uneducated youth. He left school at thirteen and there weren't too many job opportunities available to him. The only thing going was the job of a shit-house cleaner.

"Fill out this form," said the prospective employer.

"But I can't write," said the boy.

"Well," said the prospective employer, "you don't qualify for this job, so be on your way."

On the way home, the lad bought a box of apples for $2. He sold them around the neighbourhood for $6. He developed this idea and years later, finished up with a chain of 20 fruit and vegetable markets.

One day, his bank manager asked him to sign some papers.

"Can't write," he said.

The bank manager was amazed. "You can't write? My God! What would you have been if you had been able to write!"

"A shit-house cleaner," came the reply.

***

A good looking, husky young man walked into the barber shop and asked, "How many before me?"

"Three hair cuts and a shave," replied the barber.

The young man left, but returned the next day and asked, "How many before me today?"

"Two hair cuts and three shaves," replied the barber.

This happened five days in a row. Eventually the barber sent his apprentice to follow the young man to see what he did. When the apprentice returned, he said, "I dunno, boss, he just goes 'round to your house."

***

The lonely traveller pulled into a motel and asked the reception clerk for a single room. As the traveller filled out his registration form, he saw a beautiful redhead walking across the lobby. He went over and talked to her. A few minutes later, he came back to the desk with the girl on his arm and said, "Fancy meeting my wife here! Looks like I'll need a double room now."

Next morning he came to the desk to pay his bill but was confronted with an account for $3,000.

"What's this for?" he yelled at the clerk, "I've only been here one night."

"Yes," said the clerk, "but your wife's been here for three weeks."

***

Business was bad. The boss had to dismiss one of his employees. It came down to Jack or Jill. He called Jill into his office and said, "Jill, I have to either lay you or Jack off."

"You're going to have to jack off then, 'cos I've got a bloody headache," Jill responded.

AIRLINES

The 767 was coming in to land and the pilot had forgotten to turn off the P.A. system.

"As soon as I clock off," he said, "I'm going to have a nice cold beer and then screw the arse off that blonde flight attendant."

The horrified flight attendant made a dash toward the cockpit, but tripped over a suitcase in the aisle. A little old lady sitting in an aisle seat whispered, "There's no need to hurry dear, he said he was going to have a beer first."

ALCOHOLICS

10% of all road accidents are caused by drivers under the influence. Does that mean 90% of accidents must be caused by non-drinkers?

***

"Drinking makes you look beautiful, darling."
"But I haven't had a drink."
"No, but I have."

***

What's the difference between a drunk and an alcoholic?

A drunk doesn't have to bother about going to all those boring meetings.

***

Two drunks were having an argument as to who made the best home-brewed beer. They eventually decided to send samples for chemical analysis. A week later the reply came. It said "After exhaustive tests of both samples, we are unanimous in our conclusions. Neither of these horses should ever race again."

ALL MIXED UP

Irene was suspicious that her husband, John, was fooling around with other women. They'd had an invitation to a fancy dress ball so Irene devised a plan to catch John out.

"I've got a headache," she said to John. "Why don't you go to the fancy dress ball on your own?" So John donned his gorilla suit and left for the ball.

Irene put on a monkey suit and headed off to the ball later in the night. Soon after she arrived, there was John, carrying on like a sex maniac and flirting at every opportunity. She made her way over to him and whispered in his ear, "How would you like to take me out in the garden and give me a good screw?"

So he rushed her outside and screwed her on the lawn.

Irene left the ball early to be sure she was home before John.

When they awoke the next morning, she asked him, "How was the ball last night?"

"Pretty boring," he replied. "I finished up playing cards

with a couple of other fellas upstairs. Do you remember Alan Jones? Well, I lent him my gorilla suit, and he told me that he had a great time!"

***

Scratching his head and totally confused, the gorilla left the zoo library. He had just finished reading Carles Darwin's *Origin Of The Species* and The Bible and didn't know whether he was his keeper's brother or his brother's keeper.

***

Custer's last words at the Battle of Little Big Horn: "I'll never understand these damn Indians. Just a few minutes ago they were singing and dancing."

***

Maureen was most surprised to find out that she was pregnant.

"When did you have your last check up?" asked the doctor.

"Never!" insisted Maureen. "An Italian, a Frenchman and a Yank, but never a Czech!"

ALTERNATIVE MEDICINE

Colin was completely bald and clean shaven. He was seeking a remedy from the naturopath for his baldness.

"Every night for three months, rub the secretion from a woman's vagina on your head," advised the naturopath.

In three months, Colin returned.

"You dirty bastard!" exclaimed the naturopath when he saw Colin's luxurious moustache.

***

The doctor dropped into his club most nights to have his favourite cocktail, an almond daquiri.

One night, Dick the bartender found he was out of almonds, so he added some crushed hickory nuts instead.

The doctor took one sip and beckoned to the barman. "Is this an almond daquiri, Dick?"

"No," said Dick, "it's a hickory daquiri Doc."

ANIMALS

Jim had been Mayor for 20 years and was cheesed off for not receiving appropriate recognition.

"See that suspension bridge?" he complained to a fellow councillor. "I not only designed it, I also put thousands of dollars of my own money into its construction. I've worked on the hospital committee, town planning committee, the school committee. And I get no gratitude or thanks from anyone! Not even 'Well Done'. Do they ever talk about me? No! ... but fuck just one sheep ..."

***

"Are you worried about this Mad Cow disease that's going about?" said one cow to another.

"No," replied the other, "cos I'm a goat."

***

The local spiritualist church was being addressed by an eminent spiritualist from overseas. After a spine-tingling talk about the supernatural, he asked his audience if anyone had had an intimate relationship with a ghost. "Come forward," he said, "and tell us about it."

A hand went up in the middle of the audience. "I have, though I'd prefer not to discuss it."

After great applause and encouragement from the rest of the congregation, the shy, introverted little man came forward and introduced himself as Timothy.

"Well now, Timothy," said the spiritualist, "tell us about your intimate relationship with a ghost."

"Ghost!" exclaimed Timothy, "I thought you said 'goat'!"

***

Johnny's parrot had just fallen off its perch and died. It was lying on its back on the bottom of the cage, its legs pointing upwards. Johnny asked his father, "Dad, when birds die, why do their feet always point upwards?"

"Well, Johnny, they do that so that God can reach down, take them by the claws and pull them up into Heaven."

Next day when Dad got home from work, Johnny rushed over to him and said, "Gee Dad, we nearly lost Mum today."

"What do you mean?" queried his father.

"Well, I heard these noises upstairs so I rushed up to see what was happening. There was Mum, lying on the bed, with her legs pointing straight up and she was yelling, 'God, I'm coming.' If it hadn't been for the gardener holding her down, we'd have lost her for sure."

***

There is a car accident, and six people are killed. The only survivor is a chimpanzee that is handcuffed to the steering wheel. The police arrive. The chimpanzee starts making signs and gestures to the police.

"I think this chimp is trying to tell us something! Do you understand what we are saying?" the cop asks the chimp.

The chimp nods his head. So they begin to question the chimp.

"Just before the accident, what were the people doing?" asks the cop.

The chimp raises his hand to his mouth and makes drinking gestures.

"Drinking alcohol?" asks the cop.

The chimp nods his head.

"What else were they doing?"

The chimp shows smoking gestures.

"Smoking dope?" asks the cop.

The chimp nods again.

"Anything else?"

The chimp makes hip-thrusting gestures.

"Having sex?" said the cop.

The chimp nodded again.

"And what were you doing during all this?" asks the cop.

The chimp grabs the steering wheel and begins to steer the car.

***

Did you hear about the transsexual donkey?

It had a hee in the morning and a haw at night.

***

A woman walked into the pet shop and asked the pet shop owner for a pet with a difference.

"How about this bullfrog? He's going out at $500."

"$500 for a bullfrog! You've got to be kidding!"

"This is a special bullfrog," said the shop owner. "It is trained in the art of cunnilingus. Just put him between your legs and he gets straight into it!"

"Wow!" said the woman, paying her $500 and heading for home as fast as possible.

At home, she removed her panties, put the bullfrog between her legs and said "Go for it!"

The bullfrog didn't budge, but croaked, "Rrrrbitt, rrrbitt."

The woman nudged the bullfrog a few more times but she could get nothing more than "Rrrbitt."

Disappointed and angry, the woman stormed back to the pet shop, asking for a refund.

"You told me this frog was trained in the art of cunnilingus, but he does nothing but croak."

"No way!" said the shop owner, "he's the best frog I've ever trained."

Incensed, the woman removed her panties, jumped on the counter and placed the frog between her thighs.

"See," she said, "I told you so."

The shop owner put his head between the woman's legs and said to the frog, "All right you little bastard, I'm going to show you just one more time."

***

If you have a green ball in your right hand and a green ball in your left hand, what do you have?

Kermit the Frog's undivided attention.

***

An elephant and a monkey had become good friends. While wandering through the jungle one day, the elephant fell into a deep pit. The monkey rushed to the nearest road and flagged down a Mercedes Benz. With the help of a rope, the Mercedes pulled the elephant out of the pit.

Some time later, the monkey fell into a pit and it was the elephant's turn to rescue him. The elephant just stood over the pit and dropped his dick down so that the monkey could climb out.

This story proves that if you've got a big dick you don't need a Mercedes Benz.

***

It was bedtime, and as the young boy snuggled under the covers, his Union shop steward father began telling the nightly bedtime story. "Once upon a time and a half ..."

***

In their daily English class, the teacher asked her young pupils for an example of the word 'contagious'. Little Adrian's hand shot up to respond.

"Last weekend, a big truck full of pumpkins nearly ran my Dad's car off the road. When it went round the next bend, all the pumpkins fell off, and Dad said it'd take that contagious to pick them all up again."

***

What's the difference between a University and a Technical College?

At University they teach you to wash your hands thoroughly after going to the toilet. At Technical College they teach you not to piss on your fingers.

***

The teacher was asking her third grade students for a three syllable word and to use it in a sentence. Several students raised their hands.

"Beautiful," said Barbie. "My teacher is really beautiful."

"Wonderful," said Susie. "My teacher is really wonderful."

The teacher was quite flattered, and then chose Johnnie.

"Urinate," said Johnnie.

"What?" replied the shocked teacher.

"Urinate, but if your tits were bigger, you'd be a ten."

***

The young man was trying hard to impress his date. He called the drink waiter over and asked for a bottle of Chateau Neuf du Pap 1985. Upon tasting it, the young man refused the bottle, saying it was a 1987 vintage from the north coast vineyards.

"Please bring me exactly what I ordered."

The second bottle was opened, and the young man took a mouthful and once again, impatiently exclaimed, "This is not what I asked for. This is a 1983 vintage, and it's from the vineyards of Côte d'Azure."

An old man was listening to the conversation from the bar. He went over to the table and said to the young man, "I'm most impressed by your knowledge of liquor. Try this and see if you can tell me what it is."

The young man swelled up with pride, took a mouthful of the contents of the glass and swilled it around.

"That tastes like piss!" he cried as he spat it out.

"You're right!" exclaimed the old man. "Now tell me what age I am and where I was born."

***

Charlie was in grade one and he went over to check the new kid out.

"How old are you?" he asked.

"I don't know," said the new kid.

"Do women bother you?"

"No," said the new kid.

"Then you are five."

***

"Dad, where do I come from?"

This was a question Dad dreaded hearing. He explained all about the birds and the bees, about sperm and ejaculation, egg and ovulation and childbirth.

"Do you understand now?" asked Dad.

"Not really," said the boy. "Angelo said he comes from Italy and Jimmy Lee comes from Hong Kong. So where do I come from?"

***

"**M**ummy, where did I come from?"
"The stork brought you."
"And where did you come from, Mummy?"
"The stork brought me, too."
"And what about Grandma?"
"Yes, the stork brought her too."
"Gee, doesn't it ever worry you to think that there have been no natural births in our family for three generations?"

***

"**W**here do babies come from, Mummy?"
"The stork brings them, of course."
"Well, who fucks the stork?"

***

The primary school teacher had just finished showing a video on sex education and was discussing the subject with her class. Little Johnny had his hand up.

"That video's wrong," he said. "My Dad's got two penises."

"Don't be silly, Johnny. That's impossible."

"It's true, Miss," he persisted. "Dad's got a little one that he pees out of and he's got a really big one to clean Mummy's teeth."

***

The teacher was asking the nature study class what they knew about birds. Johnny put up his hand and claimed that birds had spare parts.

"What do you mean, Johnny?" asked the teacher.

"Well, I heard Dad tell Uncle Bill that he would like to screw the arse off the bird next door."

***

Two twelve-year-old boys walked into the chemist shop. "A packet of tampons please," they said.

"Are they for your mother?"

"No."

"Are they for your sister?"

"No. They're for us."

"What do you want them for?"

"On TV it says if you use tampons, you can swim and dive, play tennis and ride horses."

ANNIVERSARIES

It was their first wedding anniversary, and he was lying back watching television. As she walked past, she whacked him with a magazine.

"Why did you do that?" he complained.

"For being such a lousy lover," she replied.

He thought about this, stood up and gave her a thump in the ear.

"What was that for?" she cried.

"For knowing the difference," he replied.

***

Family and friends had gathered together to celebrate the couple's silver wedding anniversary when the inebriated husband took the floor and loudly roared, "FORNICATION".

"For an occasion like this, we need more champagne!"

AROUND THE WORLD

AFRICAN

"There are three important tribes in Africa," said the anthropologist.

"Firstly, there are the Masai, who grow to 6' 6" or 195cm. They live in the pastural areas. They tend cattle. They are a very proud people. They thump their chest and cry, 'We are the Masai!'

"Secondly," he continued, "there are the Pygmy, who live in the dense forest. The Pygmy are 4' 6" or 135cm. They are hunters and a very proud tribe. They beat their chest and cry, 'We are the Pygmy!'

"And lastly, there are the Fukawi. They are 5' 6" tall and live in the lush grasslands where the grass grows 6' high. They are also a very proud people who jump up and down, beat their chest and cry, 'Where the Fukawi?'"

AUSTRALIAN

The new player from Kickadingo was having his first game, but was not getting his fair share of kicks. The coach sent a runner out.

"The coach said he will pull you off at half time," said the runner.

"Great!" said the country boy. "You only get oranges at Kickadingo."

***

An Australian gentleman is a man who gets out of the bath to piss in the sink.

***

Why wasn't Christ born in Australia?
Where would you find three wise men and a virgin?

***

In the remote parts of Australia, "Tie Me Kangaroo Down Sport" is considered a boundary rider's love song.

***

The coach of Aussie footballers was travelling through Dublin when the guide announced, "We are now passing the biggest pub in Ireland."
A voice called from the back of the bus ... "Why???"

***

What's the difference between an Australian wedding and an Australian funeral?
One less drunk at the funeral.

***

Terrence had just returned to Ireland after a holiday in Australia. His family wanted to hear about his trip. Terry told them that Australians were the most hospitable people he had ever met.
"They will share their home with you, they will share their grog with you, they will share everything," he said. "It's those white bastards you've got to watch."

Why do Aussies put XXXX on a can of beer?
Because they can't spell beer.

***

Why do Aussies wear shorts?
To keep their brains cool.

CHINESE

"I've just been sexually molested by a Chinese laundry man!" she screamed to the copper.

"How did you know it was a Chinese laundry man?" asked the sergeant.

"Because he did the whole thing by hand."

***

A man rang the Chinese restaurant to order some food.
"Can I speak to Ha-Fin?"
"No. Ha-Fin is out."
"Is that Ha-Fout?"
"No. Ha-Fout is not in."
"Well, who's that?"
"I'm Ha-Fup, the receptionist."
"Sorry, I'll call you back when you're not busy."

EGYPTIAN

Mohammed el Caribe was in the village market one day when he felt a great rumbling in his stomach. He could not control himself and let go a fart that could only be described as a triple thunderclap. Everyone in the market stopped what they were doing and stared at Mohammed. He was so ashamed that he left the village and wandered the desert for many years, too embarrassed to return to his home.

Now in his seventies, he felt that he would like to return to the place of his birth. He was sure that no-one would recognise him. Back in his home town again, he headed for the marketplace, and was surprised to see a big supermarket standing in its place. He asked one of the shoppers how long the building had been there.

"Ah!" replied the man. "This building was completed twenty years to the day after Mohammed el Caribe farted in the marketplace."

FRENCH

Two tourists wandered into a cannibal restaurant and perused the menu. It read:

Italian with garlic sauce – 5 shells

Roast sirloin of Englishman – 10 shells

Sweet and sour Chinese – 12 shells

American, hamburger style – 8 shells

Sauteed Frenchman – 30 shells

The tourists called the waiter over. "How come the Frenchman is so expensive?" they complained.

"Have you ever tried to clean a Frenchman?" replied the waiter.

GREEK

How do Greeks separate the men from the boys?

With a crowbar.

IRISH

The curfew in Belfast started at 10 p.m. At 9.30, the British soldiers were leaving their barracks to enforce it. A sergeant in charge of one of the patrols heard a shot ring out at 9.35. He soon discovered that Private Connolly had shot a man.

"It's only 9.35," roared the sergeant. "Why did you shoot him?"

"I know that man," said Private Connolly. "I know where he lives. He would never get home by 10 o'clock."

***

Two Irishmen were visiting London and were walking down Pall Mall.

"This is not such a bad place," said Sean. "Where else could you walk down the street, meet a complete stranger, have dinner with him and then be invited to spend the night at his house."

"B'golly, did this happen to you?" asked Seamus.

"Agh, no, but it did happen to my sister."

***

Irish John was complaining to his mates in the bar. His wife was pregnant again, and he already had eight kids.

"I'll bloody well hang myself if this happens again," he said.

But sure enough, one year later, John announced that his wife was pregnant again.

"You said you'd hang yourself if this happened," one of his mates reminded him.

"That I did," said John. "I got the rope, tied a noose in it and threw it over a branch of a tree, then I thought to meself, begorah, maybe I'm hanging the wrong man!"

***

The Irish Maiden's Prayer: "Dear Lord, Please have Murphy on me."

***

Michael O'Regan was on his deathbed. He had not long to go. One night, the smell of a lovely Irish stew wafted into his bedroom and the nostalgia brightened him up. He called his son.

"My last request, Sean, is to have a bowl of that Irish stew that I can smell your mother cooking."

Sean returned in a few minutes. "Mum says you can't have any. It's for the wake."

***

Why do the Irish call their basic currency the Punt?
Because it rhymes with Bank Manager.

***

Did you hear about the Irishman who went to the toilet?
He wiped the chain and pulled himself.

***

An Irish family was sitting around watching T.V. when the father leaned over to the mother and said, "Let's send the kids to a S-H-O-W so we can fuck."

***

Paddy was standing at the bar with a rottweiler at his feet.

"Does your dog bite, Paddy?" asked Mick.

"No," replied Paddy.

So Mick went to pat the dog, The dog just about tore off Mick's arm.

"I thought you said your dog didn't bite!" screamed Mick.

"That's not my dog," replied Paddy.

***

An Irish girl was stopped for speeding and taken to the police station. The policeman stood up and unzipped his fly and the girl cried out, "Oh no, not another breathalyser test!"

***

One Sunday morning after church, a pretty young churchgoer was knocked down by a truck as she crossed the road. She was hit with such force that by the time she hit the road, all her clothes had been stripped away.

The parish priest rushed to her assistance, and to preserve her modesty, removed his hat and placed it over her golden triangle.

O'Hara staggered out of the pub on hearing the commotion, pushed his way through the gathering crowd and stood beside the priest. He stared down at the naked girl and pronounced, "Begorrah! May the saints preserve us! The first thing we've gotta do is get that man outta there!"

***

The bishop moved out into the Remand Yard and came across three Irish inmates leaning against the wall.

"What are you in for?" he asked the first.

"Murder," he replied.

"And what did you get for that?"

"Life."

The bishop asked the next man what he was in for.

"Fraud," he replied. "I got 15 years."

The bishop asked the third man what was his crime.

"Pouring petrol over Protestants and setting them alight."

"And what did you get for that?" asked the bishop.

"About fifteen to the gallon," replied the prisoner.

JEWISH

What sucks but doesn't swallow?
A Jewish girl.

***

What do you call an uncircumcised Jewish child?
A girl.

***

There's a new one-hour Jewish porno movie just out.
There's 40 minutes of begging, 3 minutes of sex and 17 minutes of guilt.

***

Jewish men are the most confident in the world.
They cut the end off their dick before they know how long it will grow.

***

The Israelis had no intention of getting involved in the Gulf War. The last time they got involved with a talking Bush, they wandered the desert for forty years.

***

Simon Solomon was at the funeral of a good friend when one of the mourners remembered he owed the deceased $100.
"I am a man of his word," he said, putting ten $10 notes in the coffin.

This reminded another of the mourners. "I am also a man of my word," he said, coming forward and placing a $100 note in the coffin.

"I am also a man of conscience," said Simon. "I too owe our late friend $100." So he wrote a cheque for $300, put it in the coffin and took out the $200 change.

IRAQI

What did Saddam Hussein have in common with Little Miss Muffett?

They both had curds in their way.

ITALIAN

Mario gets a job on the farm. After a couple of days the other farmhands complain to the boss about him.

"He's weird," they tell the boss. "He sat down for lunch yesterday and produced a Coke bottle and proceeded to piss in it and then he sat there drinking it with his lunch! Then this morning he had hold of your wife's cat and was biting the back of its neck!"

The boss walked out into the field to talk to him. Mario had hold of one of the steers and was looking up its arse.

"Mario, what's the problem?" asked the boss. "Everyone's a bit worried about your behaviour."

"There's no problems," said Mario. "I justa wanna be one of da boys."

"What do ya mean?" questioned the boss.

"Well," said Mario, "I metta three Aussie guys in Italy anda they tolda me to be one of da boys ya gotta do three things. First, you gotta drinka da piss, next you gotta bite da pussy anda den you gotta listen to the bullshit."

***

How can you tell if an Italian woman is embarrassed about her long black hair?

Because she wears long black gloves to cover it up.

***

An Italian woman hailed a cab. She said to the cab driver, "I haven't gotta da money."

"How are you going to pay, then?" asked the driver.

"Widda dis," she said, lifting up her skirt.

The cab driver looked at it and replied, "Haven't you got anything smaller?"

***

Two racists are walking down the street in Rome when they pass an Italian organ grinder with a monkey. One throws a $5 note into the monkey's tin. His companion is surprised.

"Why did you do that? You've been telling me for years how much you hate Italians."

"Well, they're so cute when they're little."

JAPANESE

What do Japanese men do when they have erections?

Vote.

***

A Japanese tourist goes into the bank to cash a traveller's cheque. He is offered 85 yen to the dollar.

"85 yen!" cried the tourist. "That's robbery. Yesterday I get 80 yen to the dollar. Why do you do this?"

"Fluctuations," explains the manager.

"Fluck you Australians!" says the tourist. "I'm not going to be ripped off by this bank!"

MEXICAN

"Where's ya bin?" the dustman asked Willy.

"I bin on holidays," answered Willy.

"No – where's ya Wheely Bin?" demanded the dustman.

"I weely bin in prison, but I tell me friends I've bin away."

***

Why is the Mexican Olympic team so lousy?

Because anyone who can run, jump or swim is in the United States by now.

***

The tourist driving through Mexico got the shock of his life when from behind a cactus, out jumped a Mexican brandishing a huge gun.

"Take my money! My car! Don't kill me!" he pleaded.

"You do as I say, I no kill you," replied the gringo. "Unzip your pants, start wanking yourself. Now!"

The shocked traveller did as he was ordered. On completion of the job, the Mexican stuffed the gun to his nose and said, "Do it again, now!"

With sweat running down his face and body, he managed another effort, before finally falling exhausted on the sand.

"Right!" said the gringo. "Now, you can give my sister a ride to the next village!"

***

A tourist went to a famous restaurant in Mexico City.

"What's the special tonight?" he asked.

"Poached gonads," said the waiter.

The waiter explained that they were the testicles of a bull that was slain in the ring that afternoon.

The tourist was adventurous, and had to agree that the poached gonads were tasty and satisfying.

Next evening he returned to the same restaurant and ordered baked gonads. On his way out, he complained to the manager about the two miserable testicles served up on his plate.

"Ah, senor!" said the manager. "Sometimes the bull wins!"

RUSSIAN

When the Russians were accused of being behind the assassination attempt on the Pope the KGB said they'd thoroughly investigate the matter.

After exhaustive interviews and countless viewing of video tapes it became clear that the Pope opened fire first.

***

A Russian woman walked into an empty Moscow shop. "I see you have no vegetables today."

"No," said the shopkeeper, "this is a butcher shop. It's meat we haven't got. The shop with no vegetables is further down the street."

***

What do you call an attractive woman in Russia?
A tourist.

***

A Russian man and woman were in the same train carriage travelling across Russia. At the end of the first day he said to her, "Are you going to Moscow?"

"Nyet," was her reply.

At the end of the second day he asked, "Are you going to Gorky?"

"Nyet," she said.

On the third day he said, "Enough of this love talk – off with your pants."

SCOTTISH

What's the difference between a Scotsman and a coconut?

You can get a drink out of a coconut.

***

McGregor was on his death bed and he gasped his last words to his old friend, McTavish.

"Jock," he said, "There's a bottle of Scotch under my bed. When I'm gone, will you sprinkle it on my grave? Promise me, Jock, that you'll do it."

"Och, aye, McGregor, but would ye mind if I passed it through my kidneys first?"

***

A Scotsman had a medical and was told he had sugar in his urine. So he went home and pissed on his cornflakes.

***

Have you heard the story about the Scotsman who gave an Englishman, an Irishman and a Welshman ten pounds each?

Neither has anyone else.

***

Dougal MacDonald stopped a young man in the street. "Aren't you the lad that saved my son from drowning in the loch yesterday?"

"Aye," said the young man. "Think nothing of it."

"Nothing indeed!" roared MacDonald. "Where's his bloody cap then?"

***

What's the difference between a Scotsman and a canoe? A canoe sometimes tips.

***

Sergeant Major McIntosh of the Black Watch Regiment walked into the Edinburgh pharmacy. He placed a tattered old condom on the counter and asked the pharmacist how much it would cost to repair it.

The pharmacist held up the ragged condom and inspected it closely. "It needs a good rinse out and a few holes want patching. It's ripped down one side, but I suppose we could stick that together. But quite honestly, it would be just as cheap to buy a new one."

The Sergeant Major said that he would have to think it over. The next day he returned. "You've sold us," he said. "The Regiment have decided to invest in a new one."

***

How do you identify the clans in Scotland? If you lift his kilt and he's got a quarterpounder, he's a MacDonald.

***

The Irishman had just finished screwing the Scottish girl and she was far from satisfied.

"I thought Irishmen were supposed to be big and thick," she complained.

"And I thought the Scots were tight," he replied.

SWEDISH

Olaf and Inge were applying for a marriage licence.

"Name?" asked the clerk.

"Olaf Olssen."

"And yours, miss?"

"Inge Olssen."

"Any connection?"

Inge blushed. "Only vunce, when he yumped me."

U.K.

How does an Englishman know that his wife is dead?

Sex is still the same, but the dishes are piling up in the sink.

***

Two Englishmen, two Scotsmen, two Welshmen and two Irishmen were stranded on a desert island. It wasn't long before the two Scotsmen started a Caledonian Club and were playing bagpipes, tossing the caber and eating haggis.

The two Welshmen started an Eisteddford and were soon competing against each other in song and dance.

The two Irishmen started a Ceilidh and downed a few pints of Guinness.

The two Englishmen went to opposite ends of the island and would not speak to each other because they had never been properly introduced.

***

At the zoo, a lion lazed in the sun, licking his arse. A tourist said to a keeper, "Pretty quiet old thing, isn't it?"

"This lion is the most ferocious animal in the zoo," said the keeper. "In fact, just an hour ago, it dragged an Englishman into its pen and completely devoured him."

"Gee!" said the astonished tourist. "Why is it lying there licking its arse?"

"Trying to get the taste out of its mouth," said the keeper.

U.S.A.

If all American women were laid end to end, I wouldn't be surprised.

***

"Yahoo!" cried the Red Indian. He had just come across a pretty young tourist whose car had run out of petrol in the Nevada desert.

The handsome young brave offered to give her a lift to the nearest petrol station on the back of his horse. She climbed aboard and they set off. She was intrigued at his continual habit of letting out loud crazy "Whoopee!" It must be an Indian custom, she thought.

When they got to the gas station, she dismounted. "Whee! ... yahoo! ... whoopee!" yelled the Indian as he rode off into the desert.

"He seemed pretty happy," said the service station owner. "What did you do?"

"Nothing," she replied, "I simply rode behind him with my arms around his waist, hanging onto the saddle horn."

"Don't you know that Indians ride bareback?" queried the owner.

***

Most people know that Spiro Agnew was an American Vice-President, but what they didn't know was that it was an anagram for Grow A Penis.

***

The Godfather in Italy had found out that one of the Family members in America was fiddling the books. He decided to deal with the problem himself and, as he could not speak English, took an interpreter with him. He had three suspects and decided to put each through the third degree to find the guilty one.

The Godfather interrogated the first suspect, holding a gun to his head.

"I'm innocent!" he cried. "I swear on my mother's grave."

The interpreter said to the Godfather, "It wasn't him. He swears on his mother's grave."

The second suspect was interrogated. He also swore his innocence and swore on the hearts of his wife and children. The interpreter repeated his denial to the Godfather.

The third suspect was brought in. He quickly broke down. "I did it!" he said. "But please, be merciful. Do not kill me. The million dollars I stole is in a suitcase under my bed."

"What did he say?" asked the Godfather.

The interpreter replied, "He said he did it, he spent all the money and he bets that you haven't got the balls to pull the trigger."

VATICAN

Don Corleone was paying his first visit to Italy. He had two appointments, one with the Pope and one with the head of the Mafia.

"Who shall I see first?" he asked his adviser.

"See the Pope first," he was advised. "You've only got to kiss his hand."

ART

Tattoos are becoming very popular these days, so the pretty young wife decided to surprise her husband and asked the tattoo artist to do a butterfly on each cheek of her bum.

"He calls me his little butterfly," she explained.

The tattoo artist looked at her little bum and said that it would take three or four visits and suggested that if she wanted the job done straight away, that he tattoo the letter 'B' on each cheek of her bum instead. The young wife was disappointed but agreed.

That night, she said to her husband, "I've got a surprise for you." She undressed, turned around and bent over.

"Who the hell is BoB?" he cried.

BACK CHAT

A woman walked into the butchers carrying a chamber-pot.

"Pounda fillet," she said.

The butcher slapped a pound down on the counter and said, "Pound ya don't."

BAR TALK

Two guys were in an English pub. They called the publican over and asked him to settle an argument.

"Are there two pints in a quart or four?" asked one.

"There are two pints in a quart," confirmed the publican.

They moved back along the bar and soon the barmaid asked for their order.

"Two pints please, miss, and they are on the house."

The barmaid doubted that her boss would be so generous so one of the guys called out to the publican at the other end of the bar, "You did say two pints, didn't you?"

"That's right," he called back, "two pints."

***

A drunk walked into the bar and ordered a beer. He gulped the beer down, banged the glass on the bar and said, "Piss."

The barmaid refilled the glass and again the drunk gulped it down, slammed the glass on the bar and said, "Piss."

This angered the barmaid, so she went over to the drunk and said, "Piss off!"

"O.K.," said the drunk, "I'll have a double scotch then."

***

Two guys were having a quiet beer in the pub after work, when in walked a punk rocker with a multi-coloured hairstyle, his hair sticking straight up in the air and the sides shaved bald.

The guys stared at the punk rocker who, noticing them staring, promptly shirt-fronted one of them and toughly said, "What's the matter pal ... you got a problem?"

Nervously the guy said, "No ... but I think we may be related."

"Why do you think that?" asked the punk.

"How old are you?" quivered the drinker.

"Twenty-two!" shouted the punk.

"Well," said the drinker "twenty-two years ago I had sex with a parrot and I think you may be my son."

***

MOVIE STARS

Paul Simon was doing his first encore at the pop concert when a big breasted brunette screamed, tore off her clothes and streaked across the stage. She was thrown out by the bouncers.

***

Did you read Anna Nicole Smith's new book?
   It's called, "How To Make $100 million With Just One Cunt Working For You."

BLONDES

What do blondes put behind their ears to attract men?
   Their knees.

***

What do peroxide blondes and Jumbo jets have in common?
   Both have big black boxes.

***

Why did the blonde cross the road?
   Never mind that. What's she doing out of the bedroom?

***

What does a blonde get when she crosses Billy Ray Cyrus with a case of the Thrush?
An Itchy Twitchy Twat.

***

How do you get a blonde's eyes to sparkle?
Shine a light in her ear.

***

What's the advantage of being married to a blonde?
You can park in the handicapped zone.

***

Why did the blonde have square boobs?
She forgot to take the tissues out of the box.

***

What does a blonde call a mushroom with a 9-inch stalk?
A Funghi to be with.

***

Why did the blonde stare at the frozen orange juice can for two hours?
Because it said "concentrate".

***

What is the first thing a blonde learns when she takes driving lessons?

You CAN sit upright in a car!

***

What do you get when you stand a blonde on her head?

A brunette with bad breath.

***

Did you hear about the blonde who swallowed a razor blade?

She gave herself a tonsillectomy, an appendectomy, a hysterectomy – circumcised her husband – gave the vicar a hare lip – cut the end off the finger of a casual acquaintance – and it was still good for five shaves.

***

The blonde was visiting a friend in the hospital when she was approached by a member of the medical staff. "Will you buy a raffle ticket?" asked the nursing sister.

"What's the raffle for?" replied the blonde.

"One of our wardsmen died last week – it's for his poor widow and three children."

"No thanks," replied the blonde, "I won't have a ticket. What would I do with a widow and three children? I'm already supporting my lover and his two kids."

***

"Not all blondes are stupid, and I can prove it!" said the blonde indignantly. "Give me the name of any American State and I'll tell you its capital."

"Missouri," called someone.

"M," said the blonde.

***

Did you hear about the man who poisoned his blonde girlfriend with a razor blade?

He gave her arsenic.

***

What do you give a blonde who has everything?

Penicillin.

***

Why do blondes wear panties?

To keep their ankles warm.

***

What's the difference between a blonde and a brick?

When you lay a brick, it doesn't follow you around for two weeks whining.

***

What's the difference between a group of blondes and a good magician?

A good magician has a cunning array of stunts.

***

What nursery rhyme did blondes learn at school?
Hump-me Dump-me.

***

The blonde walked into the hardware store and asked the young man behind the counter for a door hinge.

"How would you like a screw for that hinge?" he asked.

"No way!" said the blonde. "But I'll give you a blow job for that watering can over there."

***

Traffic cop: "Do you know you were doing over 100 kilometres an hour?"

Blonde: "But that's impossible, officer. I only left home twenty minutes ago!"

***

A leggy young blonde was on her way home. She was wearing a very tight leather mini skirt. It was so tight that she couldn't take the step up on the bus, so she reached behind and loosened the zip. It was to no avail – the skirt was too tight. She reached around and pulled the zip down a bit further but still could not make the first step. Suddenly she was lifted up by two strong hands on her bottom. She turned around and saw a young man smiling.

"How dare you!" she said.

"Well, I thought it'd be O.K. I thought by now we'd be friends, seeing you've already opened my fly twice."

***

The lovely young blonde was learning to swim and was being held afloat by a raunchy swimming instructor.

"Will I really sink if you take your finger out?" she asked.

***

The big breasted blonde always bought dresses to show off her boobs to their best advantage. Trying on a low-cut dress, she checked with the sales assistant if she thought it was too low.

"Do you have hair on your chest?" queried the assistant.

"Of course not!" replied the blonde.

"Then this dress is too low."

***

The blonde walked into the butcher's and said, "I'll have two kilos of those pissoles you've got on special."

The butcher pointed to the appropriate sign and said, "This is an R, not a P."

"That's O.K. then, give me two kilos of arsoles."

***

A blonde was browsing around the sex shop and stopped at the dildo counter.

"I'll have that one – the tartan one with the big white top," she said.

"Sorry," said the manager, "that's not for sale. That's my thermos flask."

***

He went into the newsagency and started chatting up the beautiful blonde behind the counter.

"By the way, do you keep stationery?" he asked.

"I try to," replied the blonde, "right up to the last few seconds – then I really go crazy!"

***

The blonde walked into the hairdressing salon and insisted that the hairdresser cut around the earphones of the Walkman she was wearing. The stylist did as he was asked.

The blonde returned a month later, and again asked the hairdresser to cut around her earphones.

This happened regularly for ten months. Finally, the hairdresser couldn't contain his curiosity any longer, so, while giving the blonde a haircut, he pulled the earphones out. The blonde collapsed to the floor, gasping, and within minutes, died.

An ambulance was called, but she could not be resuscitated. The hairdresser picked up the headphones to hear what the blonde had been listening to. He put them on and heard, "Inhale, exhale, inhale, exhale ..."

BUMS

Jimmy had been a jockey for thirty years and had suffered from painful piles for most of that time. This was an occupational hazard, and the remedy around the stables was a handful of cold tea-leaves inserted every morning.

Eventually, Jimmy went to see a specialist, who got him to drop his trousers and bend over.

"Mmmm, yes, I see, I see it all," said the specialist, peering up Jimmy's bum.

"What is it?" cried Jimmy. "Is there some problem?"

"No," said the doctor, "everything's O.K. You are going to meet a tall blonde, you will take a long trip and a lot of success is coming your way."

***

What did Adam say to Eve?

"Stand back, I don't know how big this thing gets."

BUSINESS IS BUSINESS

Solly had been in the clothing business with his partner, Izzy, for thirty years. He was giving advice to his son on business ethics.

"Ethics," said Solly, "is the most important thing you should consider. For instance, suppose a woman comes in and buys a dress for $90 and pays for it with a $100 note, I wrap it for her, and she is excited, and leaves the shop forgetting her $10 change. This is the big question of ethics. Do I tell my partner or not?"

***

Ruth and Rachel were walking through the park after attending a seminar on business opportunities when a large toad jumped out on the path in front of them.

"Please," pleaded the toad, "will one of you kiss me so that I can turn into a handsome Prince?"

Rachel picked up the toad and put it in her handbag.

"Aren't you going to kiss him and turn him into a Prince?" asked Ruth.

"No," replied Rachel, "Princes are a dime a dozen but a talking toad – now there's an opportunity for making big bucks!"

***

The Chairman stood to address the shareholders. "This time last year, we were poised on the edge of a precipice. Now, we are ready to take a great leap forward."

***

Solly suggested to Rachel that every time they made love, he would put a dollar into a jar. After they had been married for twenty years, Solly emptied the jar and found it contained not only one-dollar coins but five-, ten- and twenty-dollar notes.

"Where did all this money come from?" he asked Rachel. "Every time I screwed you, I only put in a dollar."

'So, Solly," Rachel replied, "do you think everyone is as mean as you?"

***

A busty woman gave a hundred-dollar bill to pay for her purchase in the dress shop.

"I can't accept this," said the salesgirl. "This $100 note is counterfeit."

"Call the police," the woman cried out, "I've been raped!"

CONDOMS

Bumper Stickers for the Bashful Condom User

1   Cover your stump before you hump.
2   Before you attack her, wrap your whacker.
3   Don't be silly, protect your willy.
4   When in doubt, shroud your sprout.
5   Don't be a loner, cover your boner.
6   You can't go wrong if you shield your dong.
7   If you're not going to sack it, go home and whack it.
8   If you think she's spunky, cover your monkey.
9   If you slip between her thighs, be sure to condomise.
10 It will be sweeter if you wrap your peter.
11 She won't get sick if you wrap up your dick.
12 If you go into heat, package your meat.
13 While you're undressing Venus, dress up your penis.
14 When you take off her pants and blouse, dress up your trouser mouse.
15 Especially in December, gift wrap your member.

102

16 Never deck her with an unwrapped pecker.
17 Don't be a fool, vulcanize your tool.
18 The right selection! Protect your erection.
19 Wrap it in foil before checking her oil.
20 A crank with armour will never harm her.
21 If you really love her, wear a cover.
22 Don't make a mistake, muzzle your snake.
23 If you can't shield your rocket leave it in your pocket.
24 Sex is cleaner with a packaged weiner.

***

An old couple went into the chemist's and the old boy asked for a packet of condoms. "We're having a dirty weekend," he said.

The chemist said, "But you're both pensioners aren't you?"

He explained that a woman over 60 could not become pregnant.

"It's not that," said the old boy. "She just loves the smell of burning rubber."

***

Why is a condom like a coffin?

Both hold a stiff. One is for coming, one is for going.

***

The deaf mute needed condoms and nervously approached the pharmacist. He opened his fly, put his penis on the counter, pointed to it and laid a $10 bill next to it.

With an understanding nod, the pharmacist took his penis out, laid it beside the other man's, grinned in triumph, grabbed the money and walked away.

CONFESSIONS

Frank had smelly feet. They were so bad, and he was so embarrassed about them, that he thought he would never find a sweetheart and marry.

One day, he met Nellie. She had a chronic case of halitosis, and to disguise it she always held a handkerchief to her mouth.

Their courtship progressed without either knowing of the other's problem. Frank never took his shoes off. Nellie never took the handkerchief from her mouth.

Eventually they married. In the honeymoon suite on their wedding night, Frank was preparing for bed. He had taken Lysol, talcum powder, Nilodor and a scrubbing brush into the bathroom in an endeavour to overcome his foot problem.

When he had finished, it was Nellie's turn to use the bathroom. She had brought her double strength toothpaste, Listerine, Fisherman's Friend and chlorophyll tablets to try and sweeten her breath.

Meanwhile, Frank was panicking in the bedroom. He had left his socks on the basin! "What am I going to do!" he said to himself. "She'll know my secret! I must confess."

In the bathroom, Nellie was thinking the same way. "I must tell him now," she decided.

She opened the bathroom door, and there was Frank.

"I have something I must tell you!" she blurted out.

"I know," said Frank, almost passing out from her breath, "you've eaten my socks!"

COUNTRY LIFE

An old man and his son had eked out a living on their farm for 40 years. One day the son won $900,000 in the lottery.

"Here's your share, Dad," he said as he put a hundred-dollar note in the old man's hand.

The old man went quiet and then said, "I've never had any money, Son. I worked hard all my life to provide for you and your mother. In fact, I never even had enough money to marry your mother."

The son considered this. "Well that's just great!" he bitched. "You know what that makes me don't ya?"

"Yeah," said the old man, "and a fuckin' mean one!"

***

The travelling salesman's car broke down in a lonely part of the country. He walked for miles before coming upon a farm house. He limped up to the front door and knocked. The farmer answered and told the salesman that he was welcome to stay the night and that dinner had just been put on the table.

"But," he said, "I must tell you that there's only two beds in the house. I sleep in one and my beautiful, blond-haired twenty-one-year-old son sleeps in the other."

"Jesus!" said the salesman, "I'm in the wrong joke!"

***

The farmer's wife was feeling lonely and neglected. There was a knock on the door. When she answered, there stood a tramp asking for a handout. She noticed that the tramp had very large shoes and she remembered that men who have big feet also have big dicks. So she invited him in.

She gave him a feed and a couple of glasses of wine then took him to bed. When the tramp woke up the next morning, he found $60 on his pillow and a brief note which said, "Buy yourself a pair of shoes that fit."

***

Farmer Green missed the bend in the road and ended up in the river. He scrambled out of the car and sat on the roof, awaiting rescue. At last he heard a car stop. It was his neighbours, Mr and Mrs Ball. "We will go and get help," they said.

Then a second car stopped. It was another neighbour, Farmer Brown. "I'm glad you came along, George," said Farmer Green. "I'd hate to be pulled out by the Balls."

***

Clyde had just got back to his hometown after completing university.

"What sort of things did you study there?" asked his friend Mike.

"I studied Logic, for one," said Clyde.

"What's that?"

"Let me give you an example. Do you have a dog?"

"Yes," replied Mike.

"Well, it's logic that you have a backyard to keep him in."

"Well ... yes."

"And if you have a backyard, you must have a house."

"Well ... yes."

"And if you have a house, you would have a wife."

"Gee, yes," said Mike.

"Well," said Clyde, "if you've got a dog, a backyard, a house and a wife, then it's logical that you'd have children."

"Amazing!" said Mike.

"And if you have children," said Clyde, "you're not gay."

Mike headed off to try his new-found knowledge on someone else.

In the bar, he bumped into Fred.

"Have you got a dog, Fred?"

"No," said Fred.

"Then you're a fuckin' faggot!"

***

The two country lads were visiting the big city.

"There's a great bar down the corner," said George. "For $5 you get this beaut cocktail called a screwdriver, then they take you out the back and you get a screw."

"Really?" replied Fred. "Have you been in there?"

"No, but my sister has."

***

A cattle station owner was having a drink at the bar in a pub in the Northern Territory. A Yank walked in and started bragging.

"Ah come from Texas," he said, "where everything's big. You call your stations big! In Texas, it takes a whole week to ride around my spread on a horse!"

"Shit!" exclaimed the station owner. "I had a horse like that so we shot the lazy bastard."

***

Bill and Jean were sitting on the bench outside the country pub watching a bull humping a cow in the paddock across the road.

"Gee, I'd like to be doin' what that bull's doin'," said Bill.

"Why don't you," said Jean, "it's your cow."

***

A city guy was speeding along a country road and, as he passed a farm, a rooster ran in front of the car and was killed instantly. The guy got out, picked up the dead bird, took it over to the farmhouse and knocked on the door. The farmer's wife answered.

"I'm sorry, lady, I've just killed your rooster and I would like to replace it."

"Please yourself," said the farmer's wife, "the hens are around the back."

The primary school teacher was preparing the class for their annual concert. Some children were to sing songs, others recite poetry and some to play musical instruments. Little Alfie had just come down from the country and the teacher asked him if he would do some farmyard impressions.

On the night of the concert, Alfie nervously walked onto the stage.

"Farmyard noises," he announced. Then, cupping his hands to his mouth, he yelled at the top of his voice, "Get off that fuckin' tractor! Shut the fuckin' gate! Get that fuckin' calf out of the yard ...!"

***

Two city blokes were watching Dave grooming his prize bull. One of them checked his watch and found that it had stopped, so he called to Dave, "Can you tell us the time?"

Dave squatted down and put his two hands under the bull's testicles, lifted them gently and said, "It's four thirty."

"That's incredible!" said one of the city guys. "You country fellas have really got a sixth sense about nature."

They wandered off, discussing what Dave had done, and just couldn't work it out. So they went back and Dave was still grooming his prize bull.

"Can you tell us the time again?" asked one of the city blokes.

"Sure," said Dave. Squatting down he carefully lifted the bull's testicles and said, "It's five past five."

"That's amazing! Do you reckon you could show us how to do that?"

"Sure," said Dave, "come over here.

"Now, squat down, gently lift the bull's balls, and you can see the Town Hall clock from here."

***

The new priest was visiting Dennis and Doris out on their farm.

"And how many children have you got?" he asked.

"Six," replied Doris. "Three sets of twins."

"That's unusual," said the priest. "Twins every time!"

"No! No!" said Doris. "Thousands of times – nothing!"

***

A farmer bought 6 sheep – 5 ewes and a ram. He asked the salesman, "How will I know when the females are pregnant?"

"Simple," said the salesman. "At dawn, look out your window. If the sheep are standing around eating, they're not pregnant. When they become pregnant, they like to roll on the grass at the crack of dawn."

So every morning at the crack of dawn, the farmer looked out of the window, and every morning the sheep were not rolling, they were eating. After a month of this he said to his wife, "This ram's no good. He's not getting the females pregnant. What are we going to do?"

"Well," she replied, "a friend of mine told me that her husband had the same problem. He put the sheep in the back of the pick-up truck, took them out to the barn and did the job himself."

Being a New Zealander, the farmer liked the idea. "Do you think it would help?" he asked enthusiastically.

"I don't know but it's worth a try," she said.

So he put the sheep in the back of the truck, drove them to the barn and did the job himself.

The next morning at dawn, he looked out the window but the sheep were still grazing on the grass. So he put them in the back of the truck again, drove them to the barn and did it again.

Next morning he looked eagerly out the window, but still the sheep were grazing. So he put them in the truck again, drove them to the barn and repeated the job.

This went on every day for ten days. On the eleventh day he woke up and said to his wife, "I can't bear to look out that window and see those sheep grazing on the grass. Will you look out and see what they're doing?"

His wife looked out the window. "Well," she said, "there's three in the back of the truck and one tooting the horn."

COURTSHIP

The young man was so nervous when he approached his highly formal prospective father-in-law that he blurted out the words.

"I am asking for your daughter's hole in handy matrimony!"

***

When the Transit Cop saw the young couple screwing away in the late night train compartment, he used his radio to notify the police, who boarded soon after.

The girl was let off with a warning, but her boyfriend was charged with mounting and dismounting while the train was in motion, and for having a first-class ride while holding a second-class ticket.

***

The young man was having his first sex experience, a quickie on the back seat of his car. After he had finished, he said, "If I'd have known you were a virgin I'd have taken more time."

"If I knew you had more time," she replied, "I would have taken off my pantyhose."

***

How do you stop a woman from giving you head?
Marry her.

***

They were both nervous on their first night together. He parked the car in Lovers Lane, put his arm around her and whispered in her ear, "Would you like to get in the back seat?"

"No," she replied, "I'd rather stay here in the front seat with you."

***

They were making love in the park. The session was getting really heavy. He was giving her oral sex. He looked up and said, "Gee, I wish I had a torch."

"So do I," she replied, "you've been eating grass for the last ten minutes."

***

The young guy was not proud of his small penis and was very shy about it. When he took his new girlfriend to bed for the first time he insisted that they turn out the lights. In the darkness, he put his erection in her hand.

"No thank you," she said, "I don't smoke."

***

"But this isn't an engagement ring. It's just a tiny, unset diamond," complained the petulant young woman.

"I know," said her boyfriend, "but it will be mounted the day after you are."

***

"**W**hat's the difference between a tram and a taxi?" he asked her.

"I give in. I don't know."

"Good. Then we'll take a tram."

ROYALTY

When Jock met Queen Elizabeth, he was overawed and didn't know how to behave. He'd only ever seen her on a postage stamp and didn't know whether to shake her hand or lick the back of her neck.

***

When Prince Andrew first got engaged to Fergie, he asked his father, "How will I know if she's a virgin?"

"It's simple, Son," replied Prince Phillip. "On your honeymoon night, when you get into bed, if she's clumsy, nervous, makes mistakes and is not sure what to do, then you can be fairly sure she's a virgin. But if she gives **you** instructions and tells **you** what to do, you'll know she's been around."

After the honeymoon, Phillip asked, "How was it, Son?"

"Just great, Father," said Andrew. "It was just the way you said ... and she was definitely a virgin."

"Was she nervous, Son?" asked Phillip.

"She sure was, Father," Andrew replied. "In fact she was so nervous and confused that when we got into bed, instead of putting the pillow under her head, she stuck it under her bum!"

***

What was Will Carling's favourite movie?

Poke-her-Highness.

***

Why did Camelot cum a lot?
He played with his lance a lot.

***

Prince Charles was opening the Birdsville Racing Carnival. He looked dashing in his Savile Row suit, but on his head, he was wearing a fur cap with a bushy tail hanging down the back.

A reporter on the local paper approached His Royal Highness and asked him why he was wearing such a hat.

"Well," said the Prince, "I was talking to Mummy last night and telling her about the beastly flies, and when I told her that I was going to the Birdsville Races, she said, 'Where the focks 'at?'"

***

Paul Keating rang the Queen. "Make Australia a Kingdom," he said, "and I'll be the King."

The Queen replied, "I will make it a country and you can stay what you are ..."

CUNNING LINGUISTS

Two Italian men get on a bus and take a seat behind a middle-aged lady. An animated conversation takes place between the two Italians.

"Emma come first. Den I come. Den two asses, dey come together. Den I come again. Two asses, dey come together again. I come again and pee twice. Den I come once more."

The lady looked around and angrily said, "You filthy, foul-mouthed swine! In this country, we don't talk about our sex lives in public!"

"You coola down, lady," said the Italian. "I'ma justa tellin my friend how to spella Mississippi."

***

Zoe was most concerned and went to see her local doctor.

"I've got green marks on the inside of my thighs," she complained to her doctor.

The doctor got her to remove her clothing and get on the couch for an examination.

"Hmm," he murmured. "I've seen this problem before."

"What is it?" cried Zoe.

"Have you had sex with a gypsy?" asked the doctor.

"Well, yes, I have," confessed Zoe.

"That's the problem," said the doctor. "Next time you see him, tell him his earrings aren't made of gold."

***

Cunnilingus: A real tongue twister.

***

A white guy is having a leak at a hotel urinal when two black guys walk in to take a leak. He glances down and notices that their dicks are no bigger than his and one of them has a white dick. "Hey, I'm disappointed with you guys," says the white fellow to one of the blacks. "You've got such a big reputation about your dicks but they're the same size as mine and your friend has a white one!"

"We're not black, we're white," says the first black man. "We work in the coal mines and he goes home for lunch."

114

ARMY

Private Maguire was in charge of the motor pool. The phone rang and an authoritative voice demanded to know how many vehicles were operational at that moment.

"We've got five trucks, a semi trailer, eight utilities, twelve staff cars and a Rolls Royce that that pompous alcoholic old colonel swans around in."

"Do you know who you're speaking to?" demanded the voice.

"No," replied Private Maguire.

"It's that pompous alcoholic old colonel you referred to."

"Well," said Private Maguire. "Do you know who you're talking to?"

"No!" roared the colonel.

"Well, thank God for that," said Private Maguire as he hung up the phone.

***

At the Regimental Dinner, the colonel ate too much and drank too much, got into a fight and was challenged to a duel. His friends quickly came to his rescue and sent him home in a taxi.

Next morning, he explained to his batman, "All that mess on my jacket – some drunken bounder bumped into me and vomited all over my tunic. I'll give the blighter a month's detention if I find him."

The batman gathered his clothes, saying, "I'd make it two months, sir. The bastard has shit in your pants too."

***

Representatives of the Armed Forces had got together for a meeting and were introducing themselves.

The first took a step forward, put out his hand and said, "George Smith, General, Australian Army, married, two sons, both lawyers."

The next stepped forward, put out his hand and said, "Bill Johnson, General, Australian Army, married, two sons, both surgeons."

There was an embarrassing silence until the third officer put out his hand and said, "Jack Collins, Petty Officer, Australian Navy, never married, two sons, both Generals."

***

A young Army officer arrived in the Falklands ready to face the enemy and defend the Empire.

"Where's the enemy?" he asked the colonel.

"None of that stuff here!" said the colonel. "We've kicked the Argies out. Today is Monday – we all play tennis."

"I don't play tennis."

"Well then, Tuesday we play polo."

"I don't play polo," said the young officer.

"That's O.K.," said the colonel, "on Wednesday we have the Regimental dance."

"Sorry, sir, but I don't dance at all."

"Ah well, you'll certainly like Thursdays – that's wife-swapping night. Lots of sex and fun."

"I'm sorry, sir, but I couldn't possibly take part in anything like that."

"God, Lieutenant!" said the colonel. "You must be a homosexual!"

"I definitely am not homosexual!" replied the officer.

"Oh dear," said the colonel, "then you're definitely not going to like Friday nights either!"

***

Sergeant Dan was on patrol when he came across a quiet pool in the river. It was a hot, steamy night, so he stripped off for a swim. He was standing on the river bank when a shot rang out.

Next thing he knew, he was coming to in the recovery ward of the M.A.S.H. unit.

"What happened?" he asked.

"Well," said the surgeon, "a sniper's bullet shot your balls off. We've just repaired the damage."

Dan looked down to survey the wound. "Could have been worse," he said. "Luckily I was thinking about my wife's younger sister when it happened."

DEFINITIONS

What's Grosser than Gross?

1 Kissing your grandmother and she slips you the tongue.
2 Biting into a hot dog and it has veins.
3 When you throw your undies at the wall, they stick.
4 You're sitting on your grandfather's lap and he pops a boner.
5 Your little brother has lost his scab collection and you're eating corn flakes.
6 Finding a string in your Bloody Mary.

***

The Irish Guide to Medical Terms:

Artery   The study of paintings.

Bacteria   Back door to the cafeteria.

Barium   What undertakers do.

Caesarian section	A district of Rome.
CAT scan	Searching for pussy.
Cauterise	Making eye contact with a woman.
Dilate	To live to a very old age.
Enema	Somebody who's got it in for you.
Labour pain	Off on Workers Compensation.
Morbid	A higher offer at auction.
Nitrate	Cheaper than day rate.
Post operative	A person who carries the mail.
Recovery room	Where they do upholstery.
Rectum	Damn near killed 'em!
Secretive	Hiding something.
Tablet	A little table.
Terminal illness	Getting sick at the bus depot.
Tumour	More than one more.
Urine	Opposite to "you're out"!

***

DICKS

A man went into a jeweller's shop and flopped his dick on the counter.

Unperturbed, the blonde saleswoman looked him straight in the eye and said: "This is a clock shop, not a cock shop."

Calmly he replied, "Then put two hands on this!"

***

What's the difference between white onions, brown onions and a 30-centimetre dick?

Nothing. They all make your eyes water.

***

A man went into the Body Parts shop and asked to see the latest range of penises for sale. The salesman produced one from under the counter and said, "This six-inch model is our most popular, sir."

"Very nice," said the customer. "Do you have one a bit bigger?"

"How about this?" smiled the assistant, producing a seven-inch circumcised model.

"Yes, it's not bad," agreed the customer. "Would you have a bigger one, preferably uncircumcised?"

"Then look at this!" said the assistant, triumphantly laying a huge cock on the counter.

"That's exactly what I want!" cried the customer. "Can I get it in white?"

***

It was the first time they had made love. They were fondling each other intimately. She had his donger in her hand.

"What do you call it?" she asked. "Some guys call theirs Dick or Peter, John Thomas or Willie. What do you call yours?"

"I don't have to call mine anything," he replied. "It usually comes without being called."

***

Most men give their penis a name because they don't want a stranger making 99% of the decisions for them.

***

Sam and Geoff were standing at the urinal together. Sam peered over at Geoff and noticed how well endowed he was.

"Gee, you've got a beauty!" Sam remarked.

"Not bad, is it," replied Geoff, "but it wasn't always as big as this. I had a transplant done a couple of years ago by a cosmetic surgeon. It cost a thousand dollars."

Sam was envious and asked for the surgeon's address.

Twelve months later, Sam bumped into Geoff and could hardly wait to tell him that he'd had a penis transplant too and was thrilled with the result.

"And what's·more," said Sam, "I got mine for only $500."

Geoff was shocked, and felt that he had been ripped off. He asked Sam if he could have a look. Sam dropped his strides and Geoff studied the transplant. He looked up and smiled.

"No wonder it was only $500," he said, "that's my old one!"

***

Fred was standing at the urinal when in rushed a black man who whipped out a twelve-incher and said, "Phew, I just made it!"

Wide eyed, Fred looked over and said, "Gee, can you make me one too?"

***

What does a man with a nine-inch prick have for breakfast?

Well, this morning I had fried eggs on toast ...

***

What did Pavarotti give his girlfriend for Xmas?

An antique organ.

***

My wife calls me "Computer Man", because I've got a three-and-a-half-inch floppy.

***

What's the difference between Hard and Light?

You can go to sleep with a light on.

***

He was 6' 6" tall and was wearing high-heeled boots and a ten-gallon hat. Soon, he was approached by a woman.

"I'll bet you're from Texas," she said. "Is it true that everything is big in Texas?"

"It sure is, ma'am," said the Texan.

One thing led to another, and the Texan was invited back to her apartment. He took off his big Texas hat, and his big Texas boots, and his big Texas pants and lo and behold, proved that everything from Texas was very big.

Later, having a post-coital cigarette, the Texan asked, "By the way ma'am, what part of Texas are you from?"

MEDICAL PROBLEMS

I sent my wife in for plastic surgery – they cut her credit cards in half.

***

The registrar of the local hospital stopped the Irish intern as he was about to enter the ward with a jug of boiling water.

"No! No! I told you to prick his boil," shouted the agitated registrar.

***

How do you get herpes in hospital?
On crutches.

***

After much soul-searching and having determined the husband was infertile, the childless couple decided to try artificial insemination.

So the woman made an appointment at the clinic, where she was told to undress from the waist down, get on the table and place her feet in the gynaecological stirrups.

She was feeling rather awkward about the whole procedure, and when the doctor came in, her anxiety was not diminished by the sight of him pulling down his pants.

"Wait a minute! What's going on here!" she yelped, pulling herself up to a sitting position.

"You want to get pregnant?" asked the doctor breezily.

The patient nodded, wide-eyed.

"Well, we're out of the bottled stuff, so you'll have to settle for draught."

***

There's a new operation where they can change a woman into a man. It's called Addadictome.

***

The nurse at the Pathology Clinic was getting a bit beyond it. She was approaching retirement and was continually getting things mixed up.

One day, a young man came to the laboratory for a blood test. After half an hour, the pathologist looked in on the nurse and his patient. There she was, stroking the young man's erection.

"No!" shouted the pathologist. "Stop it! I said, prick his finger!"

***

Woman: "Quickly! I need to see an Outern."

Doctor: "You mean an Intern?"

Woman: "Have it your way, but I need a contamination."

Doctor: "You mean an examination?"

Woman: "Yes, quick, I want to go to the Fraternity Ward."

Doctor: "You mean the Maternity Ward, don't you?"

123

Woman: "What the hell. Outern – Intern, Contamination – Examination, Fraternity – Maternity. All I know is that I haven't demonstrated for nine months, so I must be stagnant."

***

The young country doctor thought his wife might be embarrassed if he told her that the lecture he was giving to the Young Country Women's Club was on sex in marriage, so he told her he would be speaking on sailing.

The following day, a bright young lady who was at the meeting stopped his wife in the street and congratulated her on the doctor's lecture.

"You're lucky having such an expert for a husband," she said.

"An expert!" replied the doctor's wife. "He's only done it twice. First time he got seasick and the second time blew his hat off!"

***

There was a nurse who liked boating so much that she spent most of her time going down on the docs.

***

The preacher was really warming up his audience.

"Hallelujiah, brothers and sisters. Let's pray for the sick and disabled. Is there anyone in the congregation tonight who wants to be healed by prayer?"

Two young men approached the stage, one on crutches.

"What is your name and problem, brother?" asked the preacher of the first young man.

"My name is Henry. I was struck down by MS when I was a child and have not walked without the aid of crutches since that day."

"Stand behind that screen, and we will pray for your healing," said the preacher, turning to the second young man.

"And your name and affliction?" he asked.

"M..m..m..m..my na.n..name's P..P..P..Peter. I..I....I've st..st..st..st..stuttered a..a..all my l..l.l.life."

"Stand behind the screen with brother Henry!" cried the preacher.

Then, turning to his congregation, the preacher implored them, "Hallelujiah, brothers and sisters, let us pray that Henry and Peter are healed. Get down on your hands and knees and pray, pray to the Almighty, that they shall be rid of their afflictions and that the Devil is cast out of their bodies.

"Henry – throw away those crutches," the preacher commanded.

Henry's crutches came sailing out from behind the screen.

"Peter – speak to us!"

"H..H..H..Henry's f..f..f..fallen o..o..over."

***

The old sailor had a wooden leg, a hook on his right arm and a black patch over one eye. "Aye, matey. These be old war wounds," he said. "I lost me leg to a cannon ball and me right hand in a sword fight."

"And how did you lose your eye?"

"I was up in the riggin' when a seagull shit in me eye. I was hangin' on with me good hand and I wasn't use to havin' the hook in the other ..."

***

Why was the leper caught speeding?
Because he couldn't take his foot off the accelerator.

***

Dr Jim had just informed his patient that he had only three more minutes to live. The patient looked up wistfully and said, "There must be something you can do for me!"

"Well," replied the doctor, "I could boil you an egg ..."

***

"I've got good news and bad news. What do you want first?"

"The bad news, doc."

"You have three weeks to live."

"What's the hell's the good news?"

"See that blonde nurse over there with the big tits? I'm screwing the arse off her tonight."

***

The doctor was doing his ward rounds.

"I've got some good news and some bad news for you, Mike. What do you want first?"

"Give me the bad news," replied Mike.

"I had to amputate both your legs."

"My God! What's the good news?"

"The man in the next bed wants to buy your slippers."

***

"Well, Mr Smith. I've got good news and bad news."

"What's the bad news?"

"Well, we've amputated the wrong leg."

"What! What's the good news?"

"Your bad leg is getting better."

***

DISAPPOINTMENT

The loneliness of a middle-aged widow and widower eventually blossomed into love and then marriage, but the wedding night turned out to be a real disaster.

"You just don't fulfil my sexual expectations," the bride commented next morning.

"You're right about that," replied her new husband, "but when I promised to fill the void in your life, I had no idea it would be so large."

***

"Doctor, doctor. I need some pills. I've become a klepto-maniac."

"Try these," said the doctor, "and if they don't work, get me a C.D. player."

***

"Doctor, doctor. Every time I sit down, I see visions of Mickey Mouse and Pluto. And when I stand up, I see Donald Duck."

"How long have you been having these Disney spells?"

***

A couple went to the doctor's surgery. The man said, "Will you watch us have sexual intercourse and give us some advice?"

"Go ahead," said the doctor.

When the couple had finished, the doctor said, "There's nothing wrong with the way you do it," and charged them $35.

This happened several weeks in a row. The couple would make an appointment, have intercourse a different way each time, pay the doctor and leave.

After a couple of months, the doctor asked, "What exactly are you trying to find out?"

"Well," said the man, "she's married, so we can't go to her house. I'm married, so we can't go to my house. The Holiday Inn charges $180 for a room. The Hilton charges $195. Here, we can do it for $35 and get back $30 from medical insurance!"

***

She was beautiful, blonde and buxom, with a baby in her arms. He was in his first day in private practice.

"What's the problem?" he asked.

"It's the baby," she said, "he seems undernourished."

Eagerly the doctor carried out an extensive examination of the baby and asked, "Is he breast fed?"

"Yes," she replied.

"Then I'd better check you. Strip off to the waist."

Embarrassed, she took off her blouse and bra, revealing a perfect pair of firm breasts. The young doctor eagerly weighed each one in his hand, stroked the nipples and lightly squeezed them.

"Ah!" he said. "That's the problem, you haven't got any milk!"

"That's not a problem," she replied, "I'm just the babysitter, but it's been very nice to meet you."

***

"Doctor, doctor, where will I put my clothes?"

"Put them over there, next to mine."

***

"I've got a gastric problem, doc."

"Do you use your bowels regularly?"

"Yes, every morning at eight o'clock."

"Well, what's your problem?"

"I don't get up till nine."

***

The doctor was caught in bed with the farmer's wife and explained to the shocked husband that he was only taking her temperature.

The farmer took his shotgun off the wall, primed it and said grimly, "I guess you know what you're doing, doc, but that thing had better have numbers on it when you take it out."

DRUNKS

The drunk staggered up the driveway of his home, where his son was working under the bonnet of his car.

"What's wrong, Son?" he asked.

"Piston broke," came the reply.

"So am I," muttered his father as he stumbled off.

***

A cab driver picked up a drunk. The drunk climbed into the back seat. "Do you have room for a crayfish and six bottles in the front?" he asked.

"Sure," said the cab driver.

So the drunk leaned over and threw up.

***

The punter had been in the bar too long. As he staggered out, he saw a sign that said, "Lunch. 12 to 1".

"Not bad odds!" he thought.

He staggered over to the barman and muttered, "Shcush me, I wanna putsch a bet on lunch."

"You're drunk," said the barman, "get out of here before I throw you out."

The drunk staggered down the street to the next pub, where he saw another sign, "Lunch. 11 to 2". He panicked. "The odds are falling! I'd better get my bet on." He staggered up to the barman and muttered, "I wanna back lunch at 11 to 2."

"You're drunk," yelled the barman. "Get out of here!"

He staggered further down the street till he came to another pub where he saw another sign which read, "Lunch. 1 to 2".

"Odds on favourite!" he thought. "No value in that. But I'll go in and see how the race finishes."

As he walked through the bar door, the barman yelled out to the cook, "Hamburger, one."

"Shit!" said the drunk. "Just as well I didn't back lunch!"

***

First drunk: "I'll never forget the day I turned to the bottle as a substitute for a woman."

Second drunk: "Why, what happened?"

First drunk: "I got my prick stuck in the neck."

***

The drunk was standing in the car park with his car keys in his hand.

"Someone's stolen my car," he slurred to a passing police constable.

"Where did you leave it?" asked the constable.

"At the end of this key," said the drunk.

"You're a drunken mess," said the policeman. "Why is your fly open?"

The drunk looked down. "And they've stolen my girl-friend too," he muttered.

***

First drunk: "I didn't have sex with my wife before I got married. Did you?"

Second drunk: "I can't remember. What was her maiden name?"

***

George went into the bar for a drink one night after work and he noticed a man in the corner passed out over his beer. He went over to check him out. The man was drunk and incoherent. George decided to do his good deed for the day, checked the man's wallet and found his address. George kept trying to help the man stand up, but he kept falling to the floor. Dragging and heaving, he finally carried the drunk outside and put him in his car. When George reached the drunk's house, he pulled him out of the car and tried to help him to the front door but the drunk kept collapsing in a heap.

George sought help from a passerby and knocked on the drunk's door, which was answered by a pleasant-looking woman. George explained that he had brought her husband home.

"Thank you," she said, "but where's his wheelchair?"

***

FACTS OF LIFE

Maurice arrived home unexpectedly. He went up the stairs and burst into the bedroom, to find a strange man lying naked in bed with his wife.

"I'll kill the bastard," said Maurice, reaching for his gun.

"No darling!" pleaded his wife. "You see the red sports car in the drive? This man gave me the money to buy it. Those golf clubs I gave you for your birthday last week? This man gave me the money. And you know how we paid off the mortgage last month? The money came from this man."

"For Christsake's woman – cover him up so he doesn't get a cold."

***

Husband comes home and finds a man bonking his wife in bed. She pleads with him. "He's been unemployed for months. He looked so miserable. He knocked on the door and asked for something to eat so I gave him the quiche that you didn't want. He had no shoes, so I gave him a pair that you wouldn't wear. Then he asked if there was anything else my husband didn't use ..."

FAIRY TALES

Red Riding Hood is tripping merrily through the forest when out jumps the big bad wolf and says, "Aha, Red Riding Hood. I'm going to gobble you up ... gobble, gobble, gobble!"

Red Riding Hood replies, "Gobble gobble gobble, that's all they think about around here. Doesn't anybody fuck anymore?"

***

What did Cinderella do when she got to the ball?
She choked.

FAITH

The boat was slowly sinking, and one passenger remained on the deck praying. A lifeboat came past.

"Quickly! Jump in!" called the boatman.

"No, I have faith in the Lord. God will save me."

The boat continued to sink and the passenger continued to pray, when a helicopter flew past.

"Grab the rope!" called the pilot.

"No," said the passenger. "I have faith in the Lord. God will save me."

The chopper moved off.

The boat continued to sink and the passenger continued to pray, when a speedboat came by.

"Quickly! Jump in! The ship is just about to go down!"

"No," said the passenger, "I have trust in the Lord. God will save me."

So the speedboat moved off.

Eventually the ship sank and the passenger drowned.

When the passenger arrived at the Pearly Gates, he asked St Peter if he could use the intercom.

"Lord," he said, "I trusted you all my life, but you let me drown. I just can't believe it."

"You can't believe it?" said the Lord. "And I sent you two fucking boats and a chopper!"

***

FAMILY PLANNING

A group of women from the fertility clinic were having a get-together to catch up on each other's progress.

"Look at you!" said one. "You must be eight months gone!"

"Yes," said the expectant mother, "but I finally went to a hypnotherapist."

"We tried that," said the first woman. "My husband and I went for six or seven sessions but it was no good."

"You've got to go alone," whispered the pregnant one.

***

A journalist for 'Woman's Day' was interviewing a mother who had fifteen children.

"And what are their names?" she asked.

"George," she said. "They're all named George."

"But what if you want to call one in particular?"

"That's easy," replied the mother, "I use their surnames."

***

Have you heard about the latest male contraceptive pill? You put it in your shoe and it makes you limp.

***

FARTS

A man goes to the doctors with a serious farting problem. The doctor listens to a few that rattle the windows and then asks him to lie on the couch.

The doctor reaches for a long pole with a large metal hook on the end of it and walks menacingly towards the patient.

"What are you going to do with that?" says the terrified patient.

"I'm going to open the window," gasps the doctor.

***

Why do farts smell so bad?
So the deaf can enjoy them too.

***

Geoff went to the doctors.

"Doctor, I've got a very embarrassing problem. Every time I stand up after I've been sitting down, I fart something awful. Funny thing is, you can't hear it and you can't smell it."

"Give me a demonstration, Geoff," said the doctor.

Geoff stood up, and on cue, let go a thunderous clap. He sat down and stood up four or five times, each time letting go an enormous fart.

"I'll book you in for surgery straight away," said the doctor.

"What's wrong?" asked Geoff, panic stricken. "What are you going to do?"

"I'll operate on your nose first, and we'll get around to your ears when we've fixed that up," replied the doctor.

***

Arthur had been in the Old Folks Home for twelve months. He was sitting in his chair, dozing on the verandah. Every time he leaned to one side, a nurse would run over and gently push him upright. This happened constantly.

Arthur's son had come to visit and ask him how he liked the home, just as the nurse raced over and pushed him upright again. "It's a nice place," replied Arthur, "but they won't let you fart!"

***

Two old ladies were discussing the merits of pantyhose.

"I don't like them," said the first. "Every time I fart, I blow my slippers off."

FINAL DESTINATION

A young man took his date to the movies to see Madonna's most shocking film. They noticed a guy a couple of rows in front, stretched out over four seats, lying there, moaning and groaning. "Ooooohh ... Aahhhh ... Ooooooohh .... Aahhhhh ...."

The couple complained to the manager, who returned with a flashlight and asked the man, "What are you doing? Where are you from?"

"Oooohhh ... Aahhhhhh ... from the balcony," he replied.

***

FINANCIAL PLANNING

Horrie had just pulled a $100,000 jackpot on the poker machine. When the club manager was presenting him with the cheque, he asked Horrie how he was going to spend the money.

"Well," said Horrie, "first I'll spend $25,000 at the race-course, and I'll spend $25,000 on wine and whisky and another $25,000 on women."

"Wow!" said the manager. "What are you going to spend the other $25,000 on?"

"I'll probably just squander that," replied Horrie.

***

An elegant woman walked into the bank to deposit a large bag of cash. The bank manager was called over.

"Did you hoard all this money yourself?" he asked.

"No," she replied, "of course not. My sister whored half of it."

***

Zeek, the bank manager, was dismissing his accountant.

"I don't know what the world is coming to. Isn't anybody honest these days?" he asked. "Where were you educated?"

"Yale," replied the young accountant.

"Such a grand university – what is your name?"

"Yim Yohansen," replied the accountant.

***

FISHY STORIES

A guy went past a seafood restaurant and saw a sign on the Specials Board which read, "Big Red Lobster Tails, $1 each." Amazed at the value, he said to the waitress, "$1 each for lobster tails! Is that correct?"

"Yes," she said, "it's a special just for today."

"Well," he said, "they must be little lobsters!"

"No," she replied, "it's the big lobster."

"Are you sure they aren't green lobsters – a little tough?"

"No," she said, "it's the big red lobster."

"Big red lobster tails, $1 each?" he said, amazed. "They must be old!"

"No, they're today's."

"Today's big red lobster tails – $1 each?" he said, astounded.

"Yes," she insisted.

"Well, here's my dollar," he said, "I'll take one."

She took the dollar and led him to a table where he sat down. She sat down next to him, put her hand on his shoulder and said, "Once upon a time there was a big red lobster ..."

GAMBLERS

Sue was playing hard to get, so Jerry played his last card.

"I'll bet you I can keep my eye on my beer whilst I go out to my car," he challenged her.

Sue knew that this was impossible so she put down $5 and said, "You're on."

Jerry took out his glass eye, placed it on the bar beside his glass, went out to his car, came back and claimed the bet.

"I'll give you a chance to win your money back," he said.

"I bet you $5 I can bite my own ear."

"You're on," said Sue.

He took out his false teeth and bit his ear lobe with them, and picked up the money once again.

"I'll give you another chance," he said. "Double or nothing. I bet you I can poke my head through this hole," he said, holding up his hand and making a circle with his thumb and forefinger. She checked the size of the hole and said, "You're on." He poked the forefinger of his other hand through the hole and touched his forehead.

"You're down $20," said Jerry, "I'll give you one last chance to get your money back. I bet I can make love to you so tenderly that you won't even feel it."

Sue knew that this was impossible, so she threw down $20 and said, "You're on!"

Jerry took Sue to the back seat of his car where he proceeded to screw her, hard and fast.

"I can feel it! I can feel it!" she cried. "You've lost!"

"Ah well," said Jerry as he continued to hump away, "you win some, you lose some."

***

The drunk was busy feeding coins into the condom vending machine and laughing as he took the packets and put them into his already bulging pockets. A young man waiting impatiently behind him asked if he could use the machine.

"No way!" replied the drunk. "I'm on a winning streak!"

***

Dennis the drunk was broke as usual but needed a drink. He knew the barman was a sporting man so he offered him a bet.

"I'll bet you the price of a glass of beer that my prick is longer than your cat's tail," he said to the barman.

The barman couldn't resist a winning bet and laid down

139

his money. He grabbed the tape measure and measured both items.

"You lose by 3 inches Dennis, so pay up."

"Not yet," said Dennis. "Where did you measure the cat's tail from?"

"From its arse to its tip," replied the barman.

"Well," said Dennis, "would you mind giving me the same courtesy?"

***

Quentin and Wally were arguing about who had the ugliest dog. Finally, a $20 bet was made. Off they went to Quentin's house to look at his dog.

"My God!" said Wally. "That's an ugly dog, but it's not as ugly as mine."

Next, they went to Wally's house. There was a paling missing from Wally's back fence, and obviously Wally's dog had taken off, so he devised a plan.

"Wait here Quentin. I'll check in the house and see if the dog's there."

He got his wife to strip off, get down on her hands and knees, threw the kangaroo rug over her and got the feather duster and shoved it up her glory hole, then asked Quentin to come in the house.

"Here she is," said Wally, "the Feather-Tailed Flock Hound."

"You win!" said Quentin. "Here's your $20. It's not the ugliest dog I've ever seen, but it's the only one whose arse-hole's on top of its tail."

***

Lionel the licensee of the country pub was known to bet on anything, even two flies crawling up the wall. One day, one of his regular customers offered him a bet.

"I'll bet you $10 I can piss in the neck of a beer bottle while it rolls along your bar," he challenged.

Lionel couldn't resist such a sure thing. "Put your money down," he said, and placed a beer bottle on the bar. His customer unzipped his fly, took out his prick, aimed with both hands, and said, "O.K., let 'er roll."

Lionel gave the bottle a push and as it rolled down the bar, his customer shuffled sideways, keeping pace with it. His aim was hopeless. Not a single drop found its way into the bottle.

"I've won!" said Lionel.

"Yes," said his customer, "you have. But I'm gonna collect $50 from each of those four guys over there who bet I couldn't piss all over your bar and get away with it!"

***

The smart young college boy was heading home on the train on his holiday from boarding school. His only companion in the compartment was an elderly farmer.

"Let's play a game," suggested the college boy.

"What kind of game?" asked the farmer.

"General knowledge. We ask each other questions and if one of us can't answer the other, then he pays a dollar."

"I like a quiz," said the old fellow, "but I don't know about the betting."

"What do you mean?"

"Well, I've spent most of my life on the farm. I'm just a simple country man and you're an educated college boy. It doesn't seem fair to me. How about if I can't answer your questions, I pay you fifty cents, and if you can't answer mine, you pay me a dollar."

The college boy was sure that he could make a few dollars here.

"I'll go first," said the farmer. "What's got five legs and flies backwards?"

"I don't know," said the college boy, slapping down his dollar. "What **does** have five legs and fly backwards?"

"Beats me too," said the farmer, "but here's your fifty cents."

***

141

GAYS

Two gays went to the fairground. Danny said he wanted to go on the ferris wheel but Bruce was too scared, so Danny went on his own. The wheel went round and round. Suddenly Danny's seat was thrown off the wheel and he landed in a heap at Bruce's feet. "Are you hurt, Danny?" he asked.

"Of course I'm hurt! Three times around and you didn't wave once."

***

Now that gays can join the Armed Forces, what is their motto?

"Never leave your mates behind."

***

Four gays were sitting in the hot tub when a blob of semen rose to the surface.

"All right .... who farted?"

***

What do you call a gay dinosaur?
Megasaurus.

***

What do you call a gay with diarrhoea?
A juicy fruit.

***

If the answer is "cockrobin", what's the question?
  "What's that up my bum, Batman?"

***

When Brooth told Thethil that his penis was twelve inches long, Thethil thed, "That's a hard one to thwallow."

***

Jeffrey: "I think my flatmate is becoming a queer."
  Johnnie: "Why do you say that?"
  Jeffrey: "He shuts his eyes when I kiss him goodnight."

***

Jeffrey: "Are you gay, Johnnie?"
  Johnnie: "No, but I once slept with a guy who was."

***

Bruce went to the doctor complaining about a pain in the arse. The doctor examined him and said, "No wonder, you've got a bunch of roses shoved up there."
  "Have I really?" said Bruce excitedly. "Who are they from? Can you read the card?"

***

The epitaph on Liberace's headstone:
  He was great on the piano but he sucked on the organ ...

***

143

Cyril the interior decorator was telling his flatmate about his exciting day.

"This gorgeous woman in a Saab convertible picked me up and drove me to her apartment," he explained. "Then she took off all her clothes and said I could have anything I wanted."

"How exciting! What did you do?" asked his flatmate.

"I took the car but none of her clothes fitted me," said Cyril.

***

What's three things a man should never say in a gay bar?

1 Bottoms up!
2 Well fuck me!
3 Can I push your stool in for you?

***

How do two gays settle a dispute?
They go outside and exchange blows.

***

John Lennon, James Dean and Liberace were sitting around Heaven, bored out of their brains. They wandered down to the Pearly Gates and asked St Peter if there was any way they could get out for a while. St Peter said he would let them go for the afternoon, but if they committed any sin during their short earthly stay, they would go straight to hell. They accepted, and with a flash of lightning and a clap of thunder, they materialised in the Red Light District in Los Angeles.

James Dean spotted a bar and headed in and ordered a

bottle of bourbon. Poof! In a flash, he disappeared the moment he touched it.

A little while later, John Lennon saw a little packet of white powder lying on the footpath. He considered St Peter's warning, hesitated, then bent over to pick it up. Poof! Liberace disappeared.

***

Two gays are walking past the morgue on a very hot day. One turns to the other and says, "Let's go in and suck a cold one."

***

What's the difference between a homo and a hobo?

A hobo's got no mates and a homo's got mates coming out of his arse.

***

A gay masochist is a sucker for punishment.

***

Gay poker is a new card game played in gay bars. Queens are wild and straights don't count.

***

GENEROUS GESTURES

A homeless deadbeat approached the well-dressed businessman and begged money for a meal.

"Have a cigarette," said the businessman.

"No, I don't smoke."

"Then come in the bar and let me buy you a drink."

"No, I don't drink."

"Here, then, let me give you this lottery ticket."

"No thanks, I don't gamble. All I want is some money for a meal."

The businessman thought for a moment. "I can do better than that. Come home with me and my wife will cook you the best meal you've ever had."

"Wouldn't it be easier if you gave me the money?" said the derelict.

"Yes," replied the businessman, "but I want to show my wife what happens to a man who doesn't smoke, drink or gamble."

***

Three old boys were discussing their families at the high school reunion.

"My son is a top computer salesman," said the first. "He topped the sales for the year last year and they gave him a brand new Jaguar," said the proud father. "But he gave it away. A very generous chap."

"That's interesting," said the second old boy. "My son's an insurance salesman. He won the sales competition last year. He won a penthouse on the Gold Coast. And he gave that away. A very generous man, also."

"And what about your son?" they both asked the third old boy.

"I'm really disappointed in him," he replied. "He turned out rather badly. He's a raving poofter and lives at Kings Cross and won't work. But I suppose he's managing quite well. Only last week one of his best friends gave him a Jaguar and another gave him a penthouse on the Gold Coast."

GET IT RIGHT

The new English teacher took her first class.

"Give me a word beginning with A," she said.

"Arseholes!" said little Johnny proudly.

Ignoring his remark, she continued, "Now a word beginning with B."

"Bastard," came the answer from Freddy.

She gave C a miss and moved on to D.

"Dwarf," said little Cameron.

With a sigh of relief she asked him to explain what a dwarf was.

"A little cunt about thirty centimetres tall!" said Cameron.

***

A husband called home at noon one day and a five-year-old boy answered. "Put your mother on the phone, Son," he said.

"She's in the bedroom with her boyfriend," said the boy.

"Right!" said the husband. "Get my rifle from the closet and shoot the both of them in the head!"

The boy put the phone down. The husband heard footsteps going down the hallway, then two shots rang out. The boy picked up the phone and said, "Okay, I did it. What will I do now?"

"Push the bodies under the bed out of sight," he instructed.

Minutes later, the boy returned. "I did what you said and now I'm all covered in blood!" he protested.

147

"Go out to the pool and wash the blood off," said the man.

"What pool?" the boy asked.

After a moment of silence, the man said, "Is this 479 5821?"

***

Jack was hurrying to get dressed, and looking forward to taking a girl from work out for the first time. His braces had broken. He couldn't find a belt. So he grabbed a pair of jumper leads from the garage to keep his trousers up.

His date looked at him curiously. "Well," said Jack, "my braces broke."

"That's O.K. then," replied his date, "just don't try and start anything!"

***

Jacko and Joe, two big brawny bouncers, were walking home from a late night out when Jacko said, "When I get home, I'm gunna rip my wife's undies off."

"Why's that?" asked Joe.

"Cos the elastic is killing me," he replied.

***

A guy walked into the chemist shop.

"I'd like some deodorant please."

"Aerosol?"

"No, under-arm."

***

The young American businessman visiting Tokyo knew no Japanese, but he nevertheless managed to persuade an attractive girl who spoke no English to accompany him to his hotel room. He felt proud of his prowess as the girl kept exclaiming "Nachigai ana!" with considerable feeling during the sex act.

The following afternoon, he played golf with a prominent Japanese industrialist. When the latter happened to score a hole in one, the American decided to make some intercultural brownie points by shouting, "Nachigai ana! Nachigai ana!" at the top of his voice.

The industrialist turned slowly, and fixed him with a penetrating stare. "What do you mean – wrong hole?"

TRANSLATIONS

Advertisement: Something that makes you think you've wanted it for years, but you've never heard of it.

Bigamist: A fog over Italy.

Condom: An item to be worn on every conceivable occasion.

Copulate: What an Italian police chief says to a constable who doesn't get to work on time.

Mine shaft: What a German calls his penis.

Pornography: Cliterature.

Red Riding Hood: A Russian condom.

Sitting pretty: Sitting Bull's gay brother.

Specimen:	An Italian spaceman.
Tear jerker:	A guy who cries while masturbating.
Vice squad:	A pussy posse.
Vice versa:	Dirty poetry from Italy.
A Virgin:	Any Tasmanian girl who can run faster than her brothers.
Incest:	Relatively boring.
Self deception:	Faking orgasm during masturbation.
Sex:	The most fun you can have without laughing.
Mistress:	Something between a mister and a mattress.
Economist:	A person who marries Elle MacPherson for her money.
Dancing:	The perpendicular expression of a horizontal desire.
Adamant:	The very first insect.
Detest:	A West Indies cricket game.
Parents:	Couples who practise the rhythm method.
Snuff:	I'm finished for the day.
Stalemate:	A husband who's lost his get-up-and-go.

GET YOUR OWN BACK

The statues of the male and female nudes had stood in the park for ages. One day they were struck by lightning and a booming voice called from the sky, "You can come alive for one hour."

The statues jumped off their pedestals and ran into the bushes where, for the next hour, came sounds of moaning, groaning and grunting of pleasure.

"Shall we do it one more time?" said the male statue to the female statue.

"Yes, oh yes!" she cried. "This time I will hold the pigeon and you can shit on it."

***

"Enough was enough!" said Bill the butcher to himself. It was fifteen years since the pretty, shy young girl had come into his shop with the news that the baby she was carrying was his. Bill had agreed to provide her with free meat until the child was fifteen.

When the child, who was now fifteen, came to collect the next lot of meat, he said, "You'll be fifteen tomorrow. You can tell your mother that this is the last lot of free meat she'll get from me. Then watch the expression on her face!"

When the boy relayed the message to his mother, she replied, "Son, go back to the butcher and tell him that I've had free groceries and free fruit and vegetables for the last fifteen years, and watch the expression on his face!"

***

"I bet I can tell you how many sheep are in your field," said the hitchhiker to the farmer.

"I bet you can't!" said the farmer.

"If I can guess correctly, will you give me an animal?"

"Sure!" said the farmer.

"There are 5,619 sheep," said the hitchhiker.

"Christ ... How did you do that?"

"I can't tell you, but can I have my animal please?"

The hitchhiker picks up an animal and walks off.

"Just a minute," called the farmer. "If I can tell you where you're from, will you give me back my animal?"

"Sure," sniggered the hitchhiker.

"You're from Dublin."

"Christ ... how did you know that?"

"I can't tell you," said the farmer, "but can I have my dog back?"

GOLFERS

Before sex, what does a woman do with her arsehole?
She drops him at the golf course.

***

I don't play golf. It ruins a nice walk.

***

Maurie was not having a good day on the golf course. After he missed a twelve-inch putt, his partner asked him what the problem was.

"It's the wife," said Maurie dejectedly. "As you know, she's taken up golf, and since she's been playing, she's cut my sex down to once a week."

"Well, you should think yourself lucky," said his partner. "She's cut some of us out altogether!"

***

A pretty young lass had just joined the golf club, and Mike offered to give her some instruction. He stood behind her and showed her how to grip the club and how to swing back and forward. Their moving bodies caused the zipper on his fly to get caught in the zipper of her skirt. They were stuck. Slowly they moved towards the club house to get assistance, when a big brown dog jumped out from behind a bush and threw a bucket of water over them.

***

Arguing about the score is not the done thing on a golf course, but here were three members going at it hammer and tongs while the fourth lay dead in a bunker. A club official was called.

"What's the problem here?" he demanded.

"Well," said one player, "my partner's had a stroke, and these two bastards want to add it to my score."

***

It was Disabled Day at the golf club, and they were playing mixed fours. Wally's partner hadn't turned up, so he wandered through the club house looking for a partner. There, sitting in the coffee lounge, was a beautiful blonde.

"I wouldn't mind playing around with her," he thought as he approached.

"I would be only too happy to join you," she said.

Wally was showing off on the first hole, and hit a beautiful wood straight down the middle.

"That's wonderful," said the blonde, "considering you're disabled. What is your problem?"

Wally took his jacket off and screwed off a false arm.

On the next hole, the blonde noticed that Wally was favouring his left leg.

"What's the problem?" she asked.

Wally rolled up his trousers and screwed off his false leg.

On the third hole, Wally hit one into the rough and his blonde partner went in with him to find his ball.

Some ten minutes later, one of the other members of the foursome headed into the rough looking for them. When he returned, his partner asked him where they were and he replied, "Wally's in there, screwing his heart out."

***

GOLF: An infuriating game that brings out the worst in people. Why was it called golf? Because all the other four-letter words were taken.

***

A husband and wife were playing golf together when the wife got severely stung by a bee. Panic-stricken, the husband ran to the club house, looking for a doctor.

"Come quickly!" he said. "My wife's been stung by a bee."

"Where was she stung?" asked the doctor.

"Between the first and second holes," gasped the husband.

"Gee," replied the doctor, "she must have a wide stance."

***

Keith, a sales representative, was taking his client, Ron, for a day out on the golf course for a quick round. After playing a couple of holes, they were slowed down by two women players in front of them.

"I'll go and ask if we can play through," said Keith.

Keith returned, visibly shaken.

"You won't believe this, Ron, but the two women in front – one is my wife and one is my mistress!"

Ron looked at his watch impatiently and said, "You keep out of sight. I'll go and talk to them."

A few minutes later, Ron returned.

"You're not going to believe this, Keith," he started ....

***

"Forgive me, Father, for I have sinned. I used the F word this morning on the golf course."

"Tell me, my son, what were the circumstances that put you under such extreme provocation?"

"I drove my tee shot three hundred metres, but the wind suddenly caught it and it landed in the rough."

"I can appreciate your disappointment. I am a golfer myself."

"No, that's not it, Father. I hit a beautiful shot out of the rough. It dropped about ten metres short and rolled into a sand trap."

"Now," said the priest, "I can really understand you using the F word."

"No, Father. I pulled out my sand wedge and hit a perfect shot. In fact, the ball hit the pin and bounced two inches from the hole."

"Is that where you used the F word?"

"No, Father."

"Don't tell me you missed the fucking putt!"

***

George was walking towards the green, and had just pulled out his putter when he heard the call, 'Fore'. He turned to see what was happening, was hit by a golf ball and doubled over in pain.

A very attractive lady golfer who had hit the ball came rushing to his assistance. "I'm terribly sorry," she said to

155

George, who was clasping his hands in his crotch. "Let me help you."

The women unzipped his fly and began to stroke his balls and dick. After a few minutes, she asked, "Does that feel better?"

"Yes," replied George, "that feels really great, but my thumb still hurts like hell."

***

A professional golfer driving his Porsche picked up an Irish girl hitchhiker. He had his golfing gear on the back seat. The Irish girl picked up something and asked, "What are these?"

"Those are tees," he said. "I rest my balls on them when I drive."

"Wow!" said the girl. "What will those car makers think of next!"

GOOD ADVICE

Every man should have a woman for love, companionship and sympathy, preferably living at three different addresses.

***

Brian had just caught his wife in bed with another man. His friend Wally was consoling him.

"Come on, Brian," he said, "it's not the end of the world."

"That's all right for you to say, Wally. How would you feel if you came home one night and caught your wife in bed with another man?"

Wally thought for a moment and replied, "I'd break his white cane and kick his guide dog in the arse."

***

If a bird craps on your car, never take her out again.

***

Pete's blood tests had been mixed up with those of another patient. The doctor scratched his head and said, "Either you've got Alzheimers or Aids."

"God!" said the patient. "What'll I do?"

"For the time being, if you can find your way home, don't screw your wife."

***

"Doctor, doctor, what's the best thing to take when you are run down?"

"The registration number of the bastard that hit you."

***

Gerry was seeking sex counselling from his doctor. His wife was losing interest in sex.

"Next time you get home from work, bring home a box of chocolates, kiss her passionately, sweep her off her feet, give her one on the lounge room rug and you will be surprised at her reaction."

When Gerry next visited the doctor, he was asked how it worked.

"Yes, she was certainly surprised," said Gerry, "and so were all the members of her bridge club."

***

DIETS

Gordon was overweight. He weighed 130 kilos. He had tried every diet and weight reduction course available. One day he picked up the weekend paper and saw an ad for the Sex Diet – "The Most Enjoyable Way To Lose Weight". He rang the number and was told that the course would cost $10 per kilogram of weight lost.

"How much do you want to lose?" they asked.

"Ten kilos," replied Gordon.

So the transaction was completed on his credit card.

"At eight o'clock tonight," said the weight loss counsellor, "one of our beautiful hostesses will knock on your door."

Gordon couldn't wait.

At eight o'clock, sure enough, there was a knock on his door. There stood the most beautiful, ravishing blonde.

"You can screw me if you can catch me," she said, and off she ran, with Gordon in hot pursuit. He didn't catch her, but by the time he got home, he'd lost ten kilos.

Next weekend, he rang the Sex Diet again. "I'd like to lose another ten kilos," he said.

"The more you lose, the more it costs," the counsellor advised him. "This will cost you $200," she continued.

"I'll take it!" said Gordon.

So a time was set for a hostess to drop by.

This time it was the most beautiful redhead Gordon had ever seen. "If you can catch me, you can screw me," she said, and off she ran, with Gordon in hot pursuit. He didn't catch her, but sure enough, he lost another ten kilos in the effort.

The following weekend, Gordon called the Sex Diet line again. "I want to lose another ten kilos," he said.

"You're getting into a very difficult area now," said the counsellor. "It will cost you $300 this time."

Forever hopeful, Gordon completed the transaction.

At the appointed time, the tallest, incredibly attractive brunette arrived. "If you can catch me, you can screw me," she said, and off she went. And she ran and ran, with

Gordon hot on her heels. He nearly caught her and he lost another ten kilos.

Next weekend, Gordon again rang the Sex Diet line and said he wanted to lose another ten kilos.

"You are getting into an impossible area," said the counsellor. "This would take drastic measures."

But Gordon had plans. He was not going to let the next hostess get away. He completed the transaction for $500.

At the appointed time, there was a knock on the door. Gordon opened the door, ready to lunge, but there was the fattest, ugliest, smelliest woman he had ever seen. She said, "The Diet Clinic told me that if I can catch you I can screw the arse off you."

***

Laurie had just returned from a tour of the brothels in Asia. He was feeling poorly and had broken out with terrible skin eruptions.

"This is serious," said his doctor sternly. "We're going to have to put you on a special diet of pancakes and pizzas."

"Pancakes and pizzas?" exclaimed Laurie.

"Yes," replied the doctor. "That's the only food that can be shoved under your door."

GYNOS

Two gynaecologists meet at golf. They discuss what cases they've had during the past month.

"Well, I had a patient with tits as big as water-melons."

"Wow! That big?"

"Yes ... that big."

"Well, I had a patient with a clitoris like a lemon."

"Yeah? That big?"

"No, that sour."

***

Most other specialists are very wary of gynaecologists. They say that they're always spreading old wives tails.

***

Have you heard about the gynaecologist who always looked up his old girlfriends when on holidays?

***

Then there was the specialist who was so good at gynaecology that he could wallpaper his bedroom through the keyhole.

***

The fat woman complained to her gynaecologist.
   "I'm just not enjoying sex any more."
   "Well," he said, "why don't you diet?"
   "Oh, will that do any good? What colour do you suggest?"

***

Patient: "Are you the gynaecologist?"
   Gynaecologist: "Yes. At your cervix, madam."
   Patient: "I am dilated to meet you."

***

"There's something wrong with my aviaries," she complained.
   "You mean your ovaries?" said the gynaecologist.
   "No," she insisted, "it's my aviaries."

"OK, have it your way. Take off your clothes, lie on the table and put your feet up here."

"You're right," he said. "It is your aviaries! There's been a cockatoo in there!"

***

She went to the gynaecologist with her problem.

"Can you stop having sex with your husband for a month?" he suggested.

"Sure," she said, "I've got a couple of boyfriends who could stand in for that long."

HEADLINES

The journalist from 'Woman's Day' was interviewing an elderly lady in the retirement home on her 100th birthday. She was still in excellent health.

"Have you ever been bedridden?" asked the journalist.

"Many times!" she beamed. "But don't put that in the magazine!"

***

Then there was the newspaper story about the four-foot-tall fortune teller who escaped from jail and the headlines ran:

"Small medium at large."

***

Leo the Lion was drinking from a stream with his bum pointing skyward just as a big gorilla was passing. The gorilla was intoxicated after eating fermenting fruit. The gorilla crept up on the lion and sunk his sausage into him. The lion let out a mighty roar and the gorilla sped off. The gorilla found a deserted hunter's camp and quickly put on a safari suit and helmet, donned a pair of sunglasses, jumped into a chair and grabbed a newspaper, hiding behind it as though he was reading. The ferocious lion dashed into the camp and asked the 'hunter' – "Did a gorilla come through here?"

"Not the gorilla that fucked the lion down by the stream?" said the 'hunter'.

"Hell!" said the lion. "Don't tell me it's in the newspapers already!"

MORE IRISH

An Irishman is walking along the beach in Sydney. There are many beautiful women lying in the sun and he'd love to meet one but they don't seem interested in him. So he says to a bronzed lifesaver, "I've been trying to meet one of these beauties and I can't seem to get anywhere. You're an Aussie, you know them. What do they want?" he asks.

"Go and buy some swimming briefs that are too small for you and then walk up and down the beach until they notice you," says the Aussie.

"Thanks," says the Irish guy and goes off to the shops. He buys some tiny blue swimmers, puts them on, goes back to the beach. He parades up and down but still has no luck. So he says to the lifesaver, "I still haven't been able to meet a girl."

"OK, I'll tell you what to do," says the Aussie. "Go to the store and buy a large potato. Put the potato in your swimmers and then walk up and down the beach. Then you'll meet girls very, very quickly."

"Thanks," says the Irishman. He goes to the store and buys a potato, puts it in the swimmers. But after walking up and down for an hour, the women are still avoiding him. So he goes back to the Aussie. "I got the swimmers and put the potato in. I walked up and down the beach. Still nothing. What more can I do?"

"Well," says the Aussie, "try putting the potato to the front of your swimmers – not the back!"

***

An Irishman goes on 'Sale of the Century' and chooses Irish history as his category.

"In what year was the Easter rising?"

"Pass," he replies.

"What's the famous stone in Ireland that you can kiss?"

"Pass," he replies.

"What's the difference between the Orange and the Green?"

"Pass," he replies.

"Good man Patrick!" says a voice from the audience. "Tell 'em nothing!"

***

The time keeper was checking the bus driver's running sheet. "What time did you pull out this morning, Paddy?"

"I didn't," said Paddy, "and I've been worrying about it all day."

***

An Irishman went into a hardware store and asked for a chainsaw that would cut six trees in one hour. The salesman recommended a top of the line model. The Irishman was impressed and bought it.

A couple of days later, the Irishman brought the chainsaw back, complaining that it took all day to cut down one tree.

"All day?" queried the salesman. "There must be something wrong with it."

He started up the saw to see if he could find the problem, and the Irishman said, "What's that noise?"

***

Paddy was having a Guinness with his mate Kevin.

"If you don't mind me saying, Paddy," said Kevin, "you should draw your bedroom blind at night. I walked past your place last night and saw you in bed screwing your wife."

"Ha ha ha," said Paddy, "the joke's on you. I wasn't even home last night!"

***

Francis O'Connor had the flu.

"Why don't you take the day off?" said one of his work-mates.

"But the boss wouldn't like it," said Francis, coughing and sneezing.

"Don't worry, he's never here on Wednesdays anyway."

So Francis took his friend's advice and went home. As he passed his bedroom window, he saw his boss in bed with his wife. He rushed back to the office and said to his mate, "That was a close one, to be sure. I nearly got caught!"

***

Three builder's labourers, an Australian, an Englishman and an Irishman, were working on Sydney's highest skyscraper. It was lunchtime, and they sat down together for a friendly chat.

"Not bloody Vegemite again!" said the Australian, opening his lunch. "Bloody Vegemite! Day in and day out. If I have Vegemite sandwiches tomorrow, I'll jump off this bloody building!"

The Englishman opened his lunch. "Jam sandwiches again. If I get jam sandwiches again tomorrow, I'll jump off with you!"

Paddy opened his lunch. "Cheese sandwiches again! If I get cheese sandwiches again tomorrow, I'll jump too!"

Next day the three friends sat down for lunch. The Australian took one look at his Vegemite sandwich and said, "Shit!" and jumped off the building.

The Englishman opened his lunch and said, "Jam!" and followed the Australian down.

The Irishman peered into his lunchbox and said, "Cheese again!" and he jumped.

Being friends, there was a triple funeral and the widows got together at the Wake. The Australian widow sobbed, "If only I'd have known he hated Vegemite!"

The English widow cried, "If only I'd have known that he hated jam!"

The Irish widow added, "Begosh and begorrah, it's beyond me. Paddy always made his own sandwiches!"

***

Paddy rushed into the bank and pointed a banana at the teller and shouted, "This is a cock up!"

"Don't you mean a stick up?" said the terrified teller.

"No," replied Paddy, "it's a cock up. I left me bloody gun at home."

***

Pat and Mick were walking along the street when Pat grabbed Mick by the arm.

"Look out, Mick," he said, "mind where you're stepping. That looks like dog shit."

Mick bent down and pushed it with his finger. "It feels like dog shit," he said.

Mick then put his fingers to his lips. "It smells like dog shit and tastes like dog shit. Pat, I think you're right. Lucky we didn't step in it."

***

Pat walked into the house with a handful of dog shit and said to his wife, "Look what I nearly trod in."

***

How do Irish count bank notes?
"One, two, three, four, foive, another, another, another ..."

***

The headstone read "Here lies the body of Sir Thomas Parker, an Englishman and a gentleman."
"Not likely," said Paddy, "no gentleman would ever be buried with a pommy."

***

How does an Irishman know if his girlfriend is wearing panty hose?
Her toes curl up when he's screwing her.

***

Paddy went to the doctors. He had two burnt ears.
"I was doing the ironing when the phone rang," said Paddy.
"But what about the other ear?" queried the doctor.
"Well, I had to phone you for an appointment, didn't I?" replied Paddy.

***

Dr Roberts was explaining to Michael O'Regan about how nature adjusted for some physical disabilities.

"For example," said the doctor, "if a man is blind, he develops a keen sense of touch. If he is deaf, he develops other senses."

"I know exactly what you mean," said Michael. "I've noticed that if a bloke has one short leg, then the other one is always a bit longer."

HIGHER EDUCATION

A university lecturer was discussing the anatomy of the male genitalia of various Africa tribes. He went on, "The Zulu tribe is known to have the longest penis."

It was starting to get embarrassing for the female students. One girl at the back of the lecture hall decided she'd had enough and walked out. She had just reached the door when the lecturer called out, "There's no hurry, Madam. The next plane to Johannesburg doesn't leave until 9.30 Saturday morning."

***

A university graduate had just arrived for his first day's work. The manager gave him a broom and asked him to tidy up the office.

"But I'm a university graduate!" protested the young man.

"I'm so sorry. I just wasn't thinking," apologised the manager and added, "I'll call someone to show you how to do it."

***

HIRED HELP

The wealthy socialite had a night out with her friends. She woke up the morning after, totally naked and with a terrible hangover. She rang for the butler and asked for a cup of strong coffee.

"Giles," she said, "I can't remember a thing about last night. How did I get to bed?"

"Well, Madam, I carried you upstairs and put you to bed."

"But my dress?"

"It seemed a pity to crumple it, so I took it off and hung it up."

"But what about my underwear?"

"I thought the elastic might stop the circulation, so I took the liberty of removing them."

"What a night!" she said. "I must have been tight!"

"Only the first time, Madam."

***

The butler had been reprimanded frequently for his behaviour with the female servants, and was given one last chance for atonement. He promised to reform. One night, however, he was not to be found when needed and after a search, was discovered in the basement buggering the pageboy.

The butler was paraded in front of the master. "I thought you had promised to reform," said the master.

"It's true, My Lord, I have turned over a new leaf – it's just that I started at the bottom of the page."

***

Giles the butler was summoned by the Lord of the manor.

"Giles, the vicar is coming for tea this afternoon. Would

you go down to the village and buy a bottle of whisky, a box of cigars and two ounces of snuff."

It was a long walk to the village and when halfway back, Giles realised that he had forgotten the snuff. It was too far to walk back to the village, so he needed to improvise. On the side of the road were three sun-dried dog turds. Giles picked these up and crushed them to a powder.

When he returned to the manor, the Lord of the house checked Giles' purchases. When he got to the snuff, he asked, "Do you smell dog shit, Giles?"

"No, My Lord."

The vicar arrived soon afterwards and immediately got stuck into the scotch.

"Can you smell dog shit, Vicar?" asked the Lord.

"Can't say I can, old chap," replied the vicar, "but then, I do happen to have a heavy cold."

"In that case, take a pinch of snuff," said the Lord.

The vicar reached out and took a sniff up each nostril.

"By jove!" said the vicar, "you do get the best snuff. That's cleared my head completely and I can smell the dog shit now."

***

Bass and Flinders circumcised Australia with a forty foot cutter.

HYGIENE

It was a rough-looking cafe but the motorist was hungry and decided to give it a try.

"What will ya have, Sweetie?" asked a waitress who looked like a wrestler.

"Two hamburgers and a hot dog," he ordered.

She went to the fridge, got two meat patties and stuck them up under her armpits.

"What's that for?" asked the motorist.

"Everything's deep frozen and the microwave's busted," she explained, "this is the only way I can thaw them out."

"Well okay," said the disillusioned motorist, "but forget the hot dog."

***

The pastry cook was sealing the edges of his pasties with his false teeth when the Health Inspector walked in.

"Haven't you got a tool for that?" he asked.

"Yes, but I save it for putting holes in donuts."

***

"We Specialise in Hygiene", said the sign at the bread shop.

The customer was delighted when she saw the baker pick up her rolls with a pair of tongs and put them in a bag.

"Untouched by human hands!" said the baker.

"Very good!" said the customer. "But tell me, what is that piece of string hanging out of your fly?"

"Hygiene!" said the baker. "When I have a pee I pull it out with the string. My hand never touches my dick."

"How do you put it back?" asked the customer.

"With the tongs," replied the baker.

COUPLES

Fred had just arrived home after a couple of hours in the bar. He was feeling pretty cocky. His wife was washing her bra.

"I don't know why you worry about those," he said. "You've got nothing to put in them."

She looked at him and said, "I think the same thing when I'm ironing your underpants."

INCEST

Dave was a country lad. Kicking the dirt and looking at the ground he said, "Dad, I'm gettin' married to Mabel. Is that OK? She's a good girl, Dad – she's still a virgin."

"Well, Dave," said Dad, "if she's not good enough for her family, she's not good enough for ours!"

IT'S A HARD LIFE

There was a young fella called Skinner
Who took a young lady to dinner
At half-past nine
They sat down to dine
And by quarter to ten it was in her.
(The dinner, not Skinner.)

Another young fella called Tupper
Took the same young lady to supper
At half-past nine
They sat down to dine
And by a quarter to ten it was up her.
(Not Tupper, some bastard called Skinner.)

***

Mick landed a job on an oil rig. One month on, one month off. Half-way through the first month on, Mick was getting lonely for female company. Nervously, he asked one of the other workers, "What do you do for sexual relief when you're out on the rig?"

"Try the hole in the barrel down in the shower room. Most of the men say it's great."

Mick cautiously tried it out and came back to his co-worker and said, "The hole in the barrel is fantastic. I'm going to use it every day."

"Not on Wednesdays," replied the co-worker, "that's going to be your day in the barrel."

***

Kevin dropped into the local bar for a drink on his way home. He met a very attractive redhead who later suggested that they go back to her flat. After a few more drinks at the flat, they jumped into bed and were having a wonderful time.

Kevin lost track of time, and before he knew it, it was 2 a.m.

"God!" said Kevin. "What am I gonna tell the wife?"

"Put a piece of chalk behind your ear and tell her the truth," said the redhead. "I guarantee it'll work."

Kevin was creeping into his bedroom when suddenly the lights came on and there was his wife, with her arms folded on her chest.

"Where have you been 'til this hour of the morning?" she demanded.

"I've been in bed with a beautiful redhead that I picked up in the bar."

"You liar!" roared his wife. "You've been playing snooker all night with your deadbeat mates. Do you think I'm stupid or something? You've left the chalk behind your ear."

***

Two crayfish were in the fish tank in the seafood restaurant. The male crayfish put the hard word on the female crayfish.

"Yes," she said, "but will you still respect me in the mornay?"

***

There was a brave Dutch lad who stuck his fingers in a dyke. So she punched the shit out of him.

***

A driver returned to his parked car and found his front mud guard damaged. Under the windscreen wiper he found a note which said, "Sorry I backed into your car. The crowd who saw me do it were most impressed when they saw me writing down my name and other particulars, but I'm not ..."

***

It was after midnight when the veterinarian answered the phone. The call was from a little old lady seeking advice about separating two dogs that were love-locked on her back lawn.

"Try using a broom handle," he suggested.

Not long after, the little old lady called back to report that the broom handle hadn't worked.

"Try throwing a bucket of water over them," advised the vet.

Ten minutes later, the little old lady was back on the line to say that that hadn't helped either.

"As a last resort," grumbled the vet, "go out and tell the male dog that the telephone's ringing for him."

"Do you think that'll work?" asked the little old lady.

"Well," roared the vet, "it's worked three times tonight with me."

***

JINX

Old Harry was on his deathbed. He raised himself on one elbow and beckoned his wife.

"Doris," he whispered, "you were with me through the Great Depression."

"Yes, Harry."

"Doris, you were with me through the worst droughts in the fifties and the eighties."

"Yes, Harry."

"And you were with me when the farm got burned out by the bushfires in the nineties. And last year, you were still hanging in there with me when the bank foreclosed on our mortgage and we lost the farm."

"Yes, Harry."

"And now, here you are with me today, when I'm just about to die."

Doris nodded.

"You know, Doris," he whispered, "I'm beginning to think that you're nothin' but fuckin' bad luck!"

JUST DESERTS

Breakfast was late and husband and wife were badly hung over from a particularly wild party the night before. Bleary-eyed, he said to his wife, "Was it you I made love to in the garden last night?"

"About what time?" she replied.

***

When King Arthur took off on his search for the Holy Grail, he fitted his Queen, Guinevere, with a novel chastity belt. It contained a little guillotine. If anybody tried to push past it, it sprung down with a mighty whack.

On his return from the Holy Land, King Arthur commanded that all the Knights that had stayed behind remove their trousers, and there was hardly a cock in sight. All except Sir Lancelot had lost their manhood.

"Lancelot, you are the only one I can trust," said King Arthur. "What will we do with these traitors? What will their punishment be? Come, Sir Lancelot, speak up. Have you lost your tongue ....?"

***

The blind man was standing on the corner with his trusty labrador guide dog. Suddenly, the dog cocked its leg and pissed on the blind man's trousers. As the warm piss ran into his shoe, the blind man pulled out a dog biscuit and offered it to the dog. A casual observer remarked, "Why are you rewarding that dog? He just pissed on your leg."

"I know," said the blind man, "I just want to find which end his head is, then I'm going to give him a good kick in the arse."

LAST RITES

Roland had been the meanest husband that ever lived, but now he was dead and his wife had got her hands on his life savings and insurance policy. His wife's friends and relatives were most surprised when she asked that his ashes be brought back to their home.

After the ashes had been delivered, she removed the lid from the urn and said, "Look at this beautiful big diamond ring, Roland. It's the ring that I always wanted."

She then took the urn into her bedroom where all her new clothes hung. "Look at my new clothes and that fur coat. It's the one that I always wanted."

She then went to the window and held the urn outside and said, "See that Jaguar in the driveway, Roland? That's the car I always wanted."

"And Roland," she said, "you know that blow job that you always wanted, well here it is." Whoooosh!

LESBIANS

What sort of timber is a lesbian's bed made of?
All tongue and groove.

***

The guy wandered up to her and began chatting her up.
"Look," she said, "will you piss off? I'm a lesbian."
"What's that?" he frowned.
"Well, see that beautiful blonde over there? I could go for her. In fact I'd love to get into her pants."
"Really?" he replied. "I must be a lesbian too."

***

"Everything's neat and tidy in there," said the gynaecologist after the examination.
"So it should be," said the lesbian. "I have a woman in twice a week."

***

What do you call a lesbian dinosaur?
Lickalottapus.

***

LIARS

Ivan was the smoothest talker in the world. He even made his wife feel sorry for the hitchhiker who had lost her bra and panties in his car.

***

Merv the Perv was sitting in the tram fantasising about a young nurse sitting at the other end of the carriage. The conductor came along collecting fares. He said to Merv, "I can see you're lusting after that nurse, I'll let you in on a secret. She loves to have sex with tram conductors. Every Friday night she comes down to the back of the tram depot and lets one of the conductors have his way with her."

This excited Merv. He borrowed a tram conductor's uniform and went to the back of the tram depot on Friday night. It was quite dark but there she was.

As he came up behind her, he realised that she must have heard him coming for she hitched up her skirt and bared the creamy white cheeks of her bum. The excitement was too much. He rushed at her, plunged in and humped away like a jackhammer.

Later, during a post-coital cigarette, Merv laughed. "I'm not really a tram conductor," he confessed. "That's O.K.," came her reply, "I'm not really a nurse – I'm the tram conductor."

LIMELIGHTERS

There was a drum roll, and the lion tamer cracked his whip. The largest, most savage-looking lion opened his mouth, and to everyone's amazement the lion tamer unzipped his fly and stuck his dick in the lion's mouth. The applause was tumultuous. There were cheers and calls for an encore.

The lion tamer went to the microphone and announced, "That act was not difficult. Anyone can do it! The owners of this circus offer $1,000 to anyone from the audience who can emulate that feat right here and now. Do we have any volunteers?"

"Here!" called a squeaky voice from the back row, and the spotlight picked up a skinny little man with a droopy moustache. He was called down into the ring and the Ringmaster asked him if he was ready. "Yes," said the timid little fellow. "I don't think I can open my mouth as wide as the lion, but I'll give it a go."

LOVERS

"**D**ad," said eight-year-old Danny, "I'm gonna get married."

Dad smiled indulgently. "Who to, Son?"

"My girlfriend Kathy next door. She's eight too."

"Found a place to live?"

"Well," said Danny seriously, "she gets fifty cents pocket money, and you give me a dollar, so if she moves in with me, we can manage."

Dad nodded. "You might be able to get by on a dollar fifty a week now, but what will you do when the children start to arrive?"

"No worries," said Danny confidently, "we've been lucky so far."

***

The errant wife was in the middle of a very passionate session with her lover when the phone rang. She picked up the phone and listened for a few minutes, and told her lover that it was her husband on the phone.

The boyfriend panicked and started to dress.

"Calm down," she said, "we've got plenty of time. He's playing cards with you and the rest of his mates."

***

"I don't know how I'm going to look my parents in the face after being made love to three times by a total stranger," said the French girl.

"What do you mean, three times? We've only done it once."

"Yes, but you're not going home yet, are you?"

LUCK

Simon Solomon was drinking in a bar in Belfast when he suddenly felt a pistol in his back.

"Catholic or Protestant?" demanded a voice behind him.

"Jewish," replied Simon.

"Well, I must be the luckiest Arab in the whole of Ireland."

MANNERS

John and Joanne were arguing with their next door neighbours, Ray and Ruth about their late-night parties, when Ray let go an enormous fart. It could only be described as a triple thunderclap.

"How dare you fart in front of my wife!" yelled John.

"I didn't know it was her turn," replied Ray.

***

MAN'S BEST FRIEND

Steve took his dog for a walk down to the local pub on Saturday night. He was having a quiet drink when the footy results came up on the television set. Steve's team had won and the dog started running in circles and yelping with delight.

"What does he do when your team loses?" asked the barman.

"Somersaults," said Steve.

"How many?" asked the barman.

"Depends on how far I kick him."

***

An accountant, a scientist, a draftsman and a union organiser were standing at the bar having a drink and bragging about their dogs.

The accountant bragged that his dog, Calculator, could solve mathematical problems. He put twelve biscuits on the floor and called his dog over.

"Calculator," he commanded, "divide this pile of biscuits into four equal heaps." The dog did so.

The scientist bragged that his dog, Test Tube, could take a litre of milk and divide it equally into four parts. He called the dog over and the dog completed the task.

The draftsman said, "My dog, T-Square, can draw geometric figures." He commanded the dog to get a piece of paper and draw a square and a circle on it. The dog performed this task.

"What does your dog do?" the three of them asked the union organiser. He called his dog over. "Show 'em your stuff, Coffee Break," he said.

The dog crapped on the sheet of paper, drank the milk, ate the biscuits, screwed the arse off the other three dogs, then claimed he strained his back on the job and went home to make an insurance claim.

***

George came home one day and found his wife in bed with his best friend. He shot his wife but gave the dog a reprieve.

***

An Alsatian went into the Post Office to send a telegram. He wrote down, "Woof woof. Woof woof. Woof woof woof. Woof woof." He handed it over the counter and the clerk studied it.

"You can have ten words for the same price."

"So?" said the Alsatian. "It wouldn't make any sense if I added another woof, would it?"

***

MICK: "My dog's called Carpenter. He's always doing little jobs around the house."

PHIL: "I call my dog Mechanic. I give him a kick in the nuts and he makes a bolt for the door."

***

All the regulars were sitting around the fire in the country pub when Roy walked in with his mangy dog. Roy bragged to all and sundry that Ralph was a very intelligent dog.

"Never gets it wrong," he said. "Reacts instantly."

All the farmers and drovers in the bar were sceptical.

"I'm not just talking about simple commands like 'sit', 'stay' and 'heel'," said Roy. "I'm talking about six-word sentences and instant obedience."

So a bet was laid – $100 to prove that Ralph wasn't capable of passing such a test. Ray matched it, picked up Ralph and threw him on the blazing fire and yelled, "Ralph! Get off that bloody fire!"

***

Roxy, a large black labrador, was sitting up in the seat at the movies, wagging his tail, growling at the villain and barking excitedly at the hero's escapades.

The man in the seat behind was intrigued. "Excuse me," he said, tapping Roxy's owner on the shoulder. "That dog is extraordinary. I've never seen anything like it."

"He surprised me too," said the owner. "He hated the book."

***

Max usually took his kelpie for a walk down to the local pub. Max was enjoying a few drinks when the results of the football games appeared on the television set. The kelpie rolled over onto his back and started whining mournfully.

"What's wrong with your dog?" asked the barman.

"He always behaves like that when my team loses," replied Max.

"What does he do when they win?" asked the barman.

"I don't know. I've only had him two years."

***

Jane went to her doctor complaining of a bad back. After trying every remedy that he knew, her doctor finally said, "Tell me, Jane, how do you have sex?"

"I always have it doggy fashion," she said.

"Ah, that's it!" said the doctor. "Why don't you try having it on your back?"

"Have you ever smelled a labrador's breath?" said Jane.

***

ALLAN: "Hey Terry, I saw a guy screwing a big Alsatian yesterday!"

TERRY: "Really?"

ALLAN: "Yeah, and you know how the tail gets in the way ...?"

TERRY: "Yeah ..."

ALLAN: "I thought so ..."

MATES

Jerry and Jack are hiking through the mountains when Jack is bitten on the prick by a snake. Jerry panics. "What can I do?" he cries.

"Get my mobile phone and dial Emergency," instructed Jack.

"My friend's been bitten by a snake," screamed Jerry into the phone. "What'll I do?"

"Was it a poisonous snake?" asked the operator.

"Yes, a tiger snake!" said Jerry.

"You must **immediately** suck the poison out, otherwise your friend will be dead within an hour," instructed the operator.

Jerry hangs up and says to Jack, "I'm sorry, pal, you'll be dead within an hour."

***

"Did you know my wife is a wrestler?"

"No. Why do you ask?"

"I thought you might've seen her wrestle."

"I haven't, but I've seen her box three or four times."

***

Wally and Joe were having a few drinks and discussing old times. Joe's wife suggested that Wally had had too many drinks and maybe he should stay the night. There was no spare bed, so Wally bunked in with the married couple.

As soon as Joe was snoring, his wife tapped Wally on the shoulder and suggested he might like to make love to her.

"No way!" said Wally. "If Joe woke up, he'd kill me!"

"Don't worry," said Joe's wife. "When Joe's had a few beers, he sleeps like a log." Wally wasn't too sure.

"Pull a hair out of Joe's bum, and I bet he doesn't move," suggested Joe's wife.

Wally plucked a hair, and sure enough, Joe didn't move.

So he got on the job and they had a delightful screw.

Not long after, she tapped Wally on the shoulder again. Carefully he leaned over and plucked another hair out of Joe's bum. Again, Joe didn't stir, so they continued on for a second round of screwing.

Next morning, when they awoke, Wally asked Joe how he'd slept.

"Not bad," replied Joe, "and I don't mind you screwing my wife Wally, but I don't like you using my arse as a scoreboard."

***

Fred was giving his bald mate Jim a bit of a stir.

"Your head reminds me of my wife's bum," he said, rubbing Jim's nude nut.

"By golly, you're right," said Jim, putting his hand on his head, "it sure does."

***

Frank and Harry had been partners for many years. They had just employed a new secretary and Frank had taken her out.

"How was it?" enquired Harry.

"Fantastic! And I don't mind saying, that she's far better in the sack than my wife."

A couple of weeks later, Harry took the secretary out, and the following morning, he said, "You're right Frank, she is better in the sack than your wife!"

***

The new slave had just joined the oarsmen in the Phoenician war ship, when one of the rowers collapsed and died over his oar. The dead slave was duly released from his chains and thrown overboard. The Slave Master strode up and down the aisle, separating the rowers, lashing each viciously with his whip. When he had finished, all the slaves laid on their backs and pissed into the air.

"What's going on?" asked the new slave.

"It's an old Phoenician tradition," came the reply. "Every time someone dies, there is a quick whip around and a piss-up."

MIXED FEELINGS

She had been left on the shelf and was resigned to a life on her own.

One afternoon as she was strolling through the park, a man jumped out from behind a tree and said, "This is a stick-up."

"I haven't got any money," she said, giving the would-be robber her handbag.

"I'm going to search you," growled the robber.

He put his hand inside her blouse and felt inside her bra – then ran his hands up and down her legs and his fingers searched inside her knickers. Finding nothing, he turned to walk away.

"Don't stop searching," she said. "I can write you a cheque."

***

She came screaming into the police station. "This guy broke into my apartment," she said. "He ripped off my clothes and threw me onto the floor. When I laid there, naked, he grabbed my purse and ran off."

"Did you scream?" asked the sergeant.

"Of course not!" she replied. "How did I know he was going to rob me?"

ETHNIC

What's the difference between a Jewish woman and an Italian woman?

The Jewish woman has fake orgasms and real diamonds.

***

A Frenchman, an Italian and an Australian were arguing about who was the best lover.

"When I make love," said the Frenchman, "I use my tongue with such expertise in foreplay that my wife rises one foot off the bed."

"You thinka that'sa good?" said the Italian. "I whisper sucha love talk to da wife and I stroke her so sensuously, that she a moans and a groans and she rises two a feet offa da bed!"

"That's nothing!" said the Australian. "After I've finished making love to my missus, I wipe my cock on the curtains and she hits the roof!"

***

The Australian politician was attending his first United Nations function in New York. He approached a group of diplomats and, in an attempt to make small talk with them, said, "Excuse me, what is your opinion of the meat shortage?"

The American frowned and said, "What's a shortage?"

The Bosnian slapped his forehead and said, "What's meat?"

The Russian shrugged and said, "What's an opinion?"

And the Dutchman asked, "What's 'excuse me'?"

***

Mr Woo often went to Phil's Greek restaurant and always ordered fried rice. Phil and his friends thought it a great joke to hear Mr Woo order "flied lice".

Mr Woo was sick of the taunts and asked his friend, an Oxford graduate, to teach him to speak English properly.

When he next went back to the Greek restaurant, Phil and his friends were waiting with their taunts.

"I'll have a large helping of fried rice, old chap," said Mr Woo.

"What did you say?" asked a surprised Phil.

"I said fried rice, you flucking Gleek plick."

MUSICIANS

Why are trombones like elderly parents?

Both are unforgiving and hard to get in and out of cars.

***

The piano player in the Casablanca bar leant across and put his hand on Rick the American's leg.

"Didn't I tell you I could make you forget that girl, Rick?"

"Yes ..." sighed Rick. "Play with it again, Sam."

***

Why are girls like pianos?

When they're not upright, they're grand.

***

The couple were sitting in the front row of the box just above the stage. During the interval, he was feeling a bit horny and asked her to give him a hand job.

After he was relieved, she threw the handful over the balcony, where it hit the second violinist on his bald head.

"Christ!" he said, "I've just been hit by a flying fuck!"

"That's justice," said the first violinist. "You've been playing like a cunt all night."

NUDISTS

The young man was showing off his new sports car to his girlfriend. She was thrilled at the speed.

"If I do 150kph, will you take off your clothes?" he smirked.

"Yes!" said his adventurous girlfriend.

And as he got up to 150, she peeled off all her clothes. Unable to keep his eyes on the road, the car skidded onto the gravel and flipped over. The naked girl was thrown clear, but he was jammed between the back of the seat and the steering wheel.

"Go and get help!" he cried.

"But I can't! I'm naked and my clothes are gone!"

"Take my shoe," he said, "and cover yourself."

Holding the shoe over her pubes, the girl ran down the road and found a service station. Still holding the shoe between her legs, she pleaded to the service station proprietor, "Please help me! My boyfriend's stuck!"

The proprietor looked at the shoe and said, "There's nothing I can do. He's in too far."

***

Colin was always sent for coffee in the nudist colony. He was the only man who could carry two cups of coffee and ten donuts.

***

Dwarves are banned from joining nudist colonies – they're always poking their nose into other people's affairs.

NEIGHBOURS

The charges were being read against the man in the dock.

"You are charged that on the 25th February you murdered your wife with an axe."

From the back of the Court someone yelled, "You bastard!"

The judge brought down his gavel and sternly demanded that there be silence in the Court.

The Clerk of Courts continued. "You are further charged that on the same day you murdered your mother-in-law with an axe."

"You rotten bastard!" came a shout from the back.

Again the Judge brought down his gavel and ordered that the interjector be brought before him.

"What's the meaning of this outburst?" he demanded.

"I'm his next door neighbour, Your Honour. Only a month ago, I asked to borrow his axe and the swine said that he didn't have one."

***

An Irishman drives into his neighbourhood garage in Dublin.

"Can you fill up the petrol?" he asked.

"No – we don't sell petrol," replied the attendant.

"Can you check my oil?" he asked.

"No – we don't have any oil," said the attendant.

"Well, what do you do?" asked the puzzled Irishman.

"We're a front for the I.R.A.!"

"Well – can you blow up my tyres?"

POLITICAL CORRECTNESS

NOTIFICATION TO ALL STAFF
REGARDING LANGUAGE

It has been brought to our attention that some individuals have been using politically incorrect and bad language during the execution of their duties. Due to complaints from some employees and customers who are more easily offended, this type of language will no longer be tolerated.

However, we do realise the importance of staff being able to properly express their feelings when communicating with others. With this in mind, the Personnel Section has compiled a list of code phrase replacements so the proper exchange of ideas and information can continue in an effective manner without risking offence to our more sensitive co-workers.

OLD PHRASE   NEW PHRASE

No fucking way
        I'm fairly sure that's not feasible

You're fucking kidding
        Really?

Who the fuck are you?
>
> *Hi – we haven't met ...*

Tell someone who gives a fuck
>
> *Have you run that by ......*

No cunt told me
>
> *I wasn't involved with that project*

You know fuck all about it
>
> *You seem perplexed*

I don't have the fucking time
>
> *Perhaps I can work late*

Who fucking cares
>
> *Are you sure that's a problem?*

Eat shit and die
>
> *You don't say!*

What the fuck do you want?
>
> *Hello – can I help you?*

Kiss my arse
>
> *So, you'd like me to help you*

He's a fucking prick
>
> *He's somewhat insensitive*

She's a ball-busting bitch
>
> *She's assertive and goal-orientated*

You wouldn't have a fucking clue
>
> *You could use some more training*

This place is fucked
>
> *We're a little disorganised today*

Stick it up your arse
>*No, thanks very much*

What sort of fuck-wit are you?
>*You're new here aren't you?*

Fuck off shit-head
>*Well, there you go!*

You're a fucking wanker
>*You're my supervisor and I respect you*

He's a dumb cunt
>*He drives a Volvo*

Ha – suck eggs
>*I wasn't here that day*

Fuck off
>*I'll look into it and get back to you*

Fuck off dickhead
>*I no longer require your assistance*

How'd ya get this piece of shit to work?
>*Well done!*

You fucking loser
>*Gee, that was unfortunate*

I don't give a shit
>*I'll certainly think it over*

Well, fuck me!
>*Golly!*

NEWLYWEDS

"**F**orgive me, Father, for I have sinned. Yesterday I made love to my wife."

The priest explained that there was nothing wrong with that.

"But Father, I did it with lust."

"That's all right," said the priest, "that was no sin."

"But Father, it was in the middle of the day."

"That's quite natural," replied the priest.

"But Father, I couldn't help myself. She leant over the deep freeze and I jumped on her. We made love on the floor. Am I banned from church?"

"Of course not!"

"What a relief. We've both been banned from Woolworths."

***

The new bride was a little confused about what to do with her husband's constant erection.

"Don't worry about it," advised her husband. "When you want to make love, tug it three times. When you don't want to, tug it three hundred times."

***

On their first night of wedded bliss, the groom took off his trousers and asked his new bride to try them on.

"They don't fit." she said.

"And never forget it!" said the husband. "In this house I wear the trousers."

She continued to disrobe. She threw him her frilly knickers and said, "Put those on."

He looked at the scanty briefs and said, "I'll never get into these!"

"You're right," she said. "And if you don't change your attitude, you never will!"

***

It was the young couple's first night of wedded bliss. They undressed each other tentatively, he admiring her beautiful body and she his fine physique. When she removed his sock, the last item of clothing, she saw that he had no toes on his left foot.

Shocked at this terrible deformity, she ran sobbing into the night, back to her mother.

"I told you what to expect," said her mother. "I've given you good sex education. What's the problem?"

"It's not that," she cried. "When he stripped off, he only had three quarters of a foot."

"Oh!" said Mother. "Why don't you finish the dishes and go off to bed. I'll be back in the morning."

***

The eighty-year-old man had gone to see his doctor for pre-marriage tests.

"I'm marrying a twenty-year-old," he said.

"Why are you doing that?" asked the doctor.

"I want a son and heir. Can you give me any advice?"

"Yes, get a lodger," said the doctor, smirking.

A few months later, the old fellow returned to the doctor.

"Is your wife pregnant yet?" queried the doctor.

"Yes."

"So you did take in a lodger?"

"Oh yes," replied the old man, "and she's pregnant too!"

A FREE LUNCH

The blonde at the next table was devouring an enormous meal.

"I'll bet her boyfriend's a taxidermist," said Bert to his wife.

"What makes you think that?" she replied.

"Well, can't you see he's stuffing the bird before mounting her?"

OBVIOUSLY ...

What's round and hard and sticks so far out of a man's pyjamas that he can hang his hat on it?

His head.

***

What's pink and wrinkly and hangs out your pants?

Your grandma.

***

Why do so many brides get crow's feet as soon as they're married?

From squinting and saying, "Suck what?"

***

What's got seventy-five balls and screws old ladies?

Bingo.

***

What does it take to circumcise a whale?

Foreskin divers.

***

Why is a joke like pussy?

Neither's any good if you don't get it.

***

Dr Watson and Sherlock Holmes were walking through the park when they passed three women eating bananas.

"Ah," said Holmes, "I see a spinster, a prostitute and a newlywed."

"Amazing, Holmes!" said Dr Watson. "How did you deduce that?"

"Elementary, my dear Watson. See how the spinster breaks the banana into small pieces before popping them into her mouth? Whilst the prostitute in the middle holds the banana in both hands."

"Yes, Holmes, but how do you know the other one is a newlywed?"

"Well," said Holmes, "she's holding the banana with one hand and thumping herself on the back of the head with the other."

OH SHIT!

The studious-looking young man in horn-rimmed glasses approached the young lady sitting on her own in the singles bar. After introducing himself, she said, "Tell me about yourself."

"I'm a nuclear physicist," he said, "and I've been working on a top-secret job for the last five years. Would you like me to tell you all about it?"

"Let me ask you a few questions first," said the young lady.

She continued, "When a rabbit poops, why does it come out in hard little round balls?"

"I've got no idea," said the nuclear physicist.

"Well, here's another one," said the young lady. "How can elephants drop square turds out of a round arse-hole?"

"I can't answer that," repeated the physicist.

"Well, why do dog turds drop like a coil of rope?" she asked.

"You've got me again!" he said.

"Well," she said, "it seems to me, you don't know shit! And you want to talk to me about nuclear physics!"

OLDIES

Charlie was a very sprightly 80-year-old. He thought he'd give the ladies at the Old Folks Home a bit of excitement and ran across the lawn naked. As he passed a couple of elderly spinsters, one said to the other, "My goodness, Annie, what was that that just passed?"

"I don't know what it was," said her companion, "but it certainly needed ironing."

***

The sweet old couple in the Old Folks Home were suffering from Alzheimers.

"Darling," she said, "would you get something for me from the kitchen?"

"Certainly, sweetheart," he replied. "What would you like?"

"Get me a pen and paper and I'll write it down," she said.

"No, you tell me. I'll remember," he said proudly.

"But you always forget. I'll write it down."

"No, I won't forget!" he protested.

She gave in.

"All right ... I want two scoops of vanilla icecream with chocolate sauce and crushed nuts sprinkled on top, and a wafer biscuit. Have you got that?"

"Yes," he replied.

"Well, repeat it to me," she demanded.

So he repeated the order.

About two hours later, he returned from the kitchen with a large plate of bacon and eggs.

"You silly old fool," she growled. "You've forgotten the toast!"

***

A couple of old boys went down to the pub.

"I've heard that stout will put lead in your pencil. Why don't we try some?" said one.

"You can," replied the other, "but I don't have anybody to write to."

***

Poor old Norm had had no visitors that day. He was in the Geriatric Ward of the Old Folks Hospital. A social worker went over to wipe the dribble off his chin and noticed a bowl of almonds on his tray.

"They were given to me as a present," he spluttered, "but I don't want them. You can have them."

The social worker thanked him, and began nibbling away on them. After she'd eaten most of them, she remarked, "It's a funny thing, giving nuts to a man who has no teeth."

"Oh, no," replied Norm, "they had chocolate around them when I first got them."

***

The old couple were sitting in their rocking chairs on the verandah of the Old Folks Home. They had had designs on each other for some time. He looked over and said to her, "Fuck you", and she looked back wistfully and said,

"Fuck you too."

Then they rocked away for another thirty minutes and he looked over to her and said, "I don't think much of this oral sex, do you?"

***

Grandpa had just told them the news – he was getting engaged to a twenty-five-year-old nymphomaniac. The family was very concerned. His eldest daughter spoke confidentially to him.

"Dad, we're most concerned that sex with a girl like that could prove fatal."

"So what?" said Grandpa. "If she dies, she dies."

***

The old couple had fallen in love at the retirement village. Eventually, he put the hard word on her.

"Oh, yes!" she said, as she hurriedly started undressing. "But I must tell you, I have acute angina."

"Well that's good 'cause you've got lousy tits," he replied.

***

Justin, the hotel check-in clerk, told the couple that the only room available was the bridal suite.

"But we've been married for twenty-five years! It would be wasted on us," said the husband.

"But if I put you in the ballroom, we wouldn't expect you to dance all night!" replied Justin.

***

ONE-UPMANSHIP

Pat and Mick were being shaved by the barber in the barber shop. The barber started to put aftershave on Pat's face.

"Don't put that stinkin' stuff on me!" exclaimed Pat. "My wife will think I smell like a brothel!"

Then it was Mick's turn. "You can put as much after-shave on me as you like. My wife doesn't know what a brothel smells like!"

***

Nigel bumped into Steve and his friend Paul at the bar where the lawyers meet on Friday nights for a drink. It was always a big night for one-upmanship.

Whilst having a drink together, a phone started to ring and Nigel stuck his thumb in his ear and started talking into his little finger. "It's the latest technology," he explained. "I've had a silicon chip inserted into my thumb and another into my little finger, and I've got a little ampli-fier in my ear. It's better than screwing around with one of those cumbersome mobile phones."

The next time they met, a phone rang again whilst they were having a drink. This time Paul answered, merely by talking. "It's the latest technology," he said. "It's the tooth phone. Not as intrusive as sticking your thumb in your ear and talking into your little finger. I've had a silicon chip inserted into a hollow tooth and another inserted into my ear."

About half an hour later, Steve bent forward, flexed his knees and let go a roaring fart.

"Are you O.K.?" asked Nigel.

"Don't worry," Steve replied, "it's just a fax coming through."

***

A pompous Englishman arrived to pick up his Australian visitor in a Rolls Royce. The Australian sat next to him in the front seat.

"I suppose, being a Colonial, you've never ridden in a Rolls Royce?" said the puffed-up Pom.

"Sure I have," replied the Aussie, "but never in the front!"

OPPORTUNITY

Two men were sitting in McDonald's having a hamburger when the town's fire alarm started to ring. One jumped up and headed for the door, the other called out, "I didn't know you were a fireman."

"I'm not," he replied, "but my girlfriend's husband is."

***

Dougal was a typical Scot. His wife Janet had just died and he wanted to place the least expensive death notice. He went to the newspaper office and wrote on the lodgement form, "Janet died".

The clerk explained that there was a minimum charge and he could have six words. Douglas added three more words: "Janet died, Toyota for sale".

***

ORAL HYGIENE

Gerry was half-way through his meal when he called the manager. "There's a hair in this spaghetti so I'm not paying for it."

Later that night the manager found Gerry giving one of the waitresses oral sex and said, "You don't seem to mind a bit of hair now."

Gerry looked up and replied, "No ... But if I find any spaghetti down here I'm not paying for it either."

PARENTHOOD

Little Harold was hopping on one foot then the other.

"I gotta piss! I gotta piss!" he cried to his mother in front of her friends.

Mother took him to the toilet and explained to him that next time he wanted to go to the toilet, he should not use those words. She said he should come in and talk quietly – "That's a whisper," she said.

Two hours later, Harold came rushing in again.

"I wanna whisper! I wanna whisper!" he said.

His mother knew what he wanted and took him to the toilet, after which he was rewarded with a candy bar.

That night the urge came on again. Harold jumped out of bed and ran to his father.

"What is it, Son?" his father asked.

"I wanna whisper, Daddy. I wanna whisper."

"O.K. Son, come here and whisper in my ear."

***

PATIENTS

A man was in a serious car accident and was so badly burned he had to be bandaged from head to toe and could only be fed rectally, through a tube.

A nurse had just served his afternoon coffee when he began waving his arms around.

"What's the matter?" she asked. "Is it too hot?"

Through his head bandages she heard his muffled response: "Too much sugar!"

Later, his wife called in to see how he was doing and asked, "How is his appetite?"

"Excellent," said the nurse. "It would have done your heart good, to see his arse snap at a piece of toast this morning."

***

Vic went to the doctors. His hands were trembling. He thought he had Parkinson's Disease. The doctor checked him over and asked, "Do you drink much?"

"No," said Vic, "I spill most of it."

PEARLY GATES

St Peter was checking entrants to Heaven at the Pearly Gates. "You must answer three religious questions," said St Peter, "to prove that you have been devout."

"Shoot," said the first applicant.

"Who spoke to God in the burning bush?" asked St Peter.

"Moses," came the reply.

"Well done. Now tell me, who was God's only son?"

"Jesus," came the answer.

"Good. The third and last question," said St Peter. "What is God's first name?"

"Andy."

"Andy?" queried St Peter.

"Yes. It's in the song ... Andy walks with me, Andy talks with me, Andy tells me I'm his own."

PUSSIES

A woman rushed up to the manager of the movie theatre and complained that she had been molested in the front stalls.

The manager calmed her down and was ushering her to another seat when another woman complained to him that she had been molested in the front stalls too.

The manager went down to the front and shone his torch along the floor where he saw a bald man crawling along on his hands and knees.

"What are you doing?" demanded the manager.

The bald man looked up. "I've lost my toupee. It fell off in the dark. I had my hand on it twice but it got away!"

***

What did one ovary say to the other?

They must be going to have a party downstairs. Two nuts are trying to push an organ up the passage.

***

Little Johnnie was learning new words.

"Mum, what's a pussy?"

Mother pointed at the cat and said, "That's a pussy."

"Mum, what's a bitch?"

Mother pointed to their female dog and said, "That's a bitch."

Johnnie wanted to confirm this information with his father.

"Daddy!" he said excitedly. "What's a pussy?"

Father pulled out the centrefold of the Playboy magazine and drew a circle around the appropriate part.

"Son," he said, "that's a pussy."

"Well, Dad, what's a bitch?"

"Everything outside the circle," replied his father.

***

A dwarf walked up to the tall blonde at the bar and said, "Can I smell your fanny?"

"Absolutely not!" she replied.

"Then it must be your feet," he said.

***

It was their first time in bed together.

"That's a little organ!" she said disappointedly.

"Sorry," he replied, "I didn't know I'd be playing in the Town Hall!"

DONALD DUCK

Donald Duck had split with Daisy Duck, and soon found himself going to a brothel.

"I'm here for a good time," he told the Madam.

"You must have a condom," she replied. "That'll be £1. Can I stick it on your bill?"

"What sort of duck do you think I am?"

***

Donald Duck wanted a divorce from Daisy.

"But Daisy's not insane," said Donald's lawyer.

"I didn't say she was insane," protested Donald. "I said she was fucking Goofy."

R.I.P.

Terri the tart was such a good-time girl that when she died they had to bury her in a Y-shaped coffin.

***

A guy and his wife were playing 18 holes of golf. It was a beautiful sunny day and they had the entire course to themselves.

When he was about to hit off at the 13th hole, he collapsed to the ground, clutching his chest, having a heart attack. Despite the fact that he was 6'2" and weighed 18 stone, she picked him up, put him on her shoulders and headed for the clubhouse.

She eventually arrived at the clubhouse still carrying her huge husband on her shoulders. Two other club members arrived and helped carry him inside, called an ambulance and sent him to the hospital.

"How could you carry such a large man on your shoulders from the 13th hole?" the Club President asked the wife in amazement. "Wasn't it difficult?"

"Yes," said the wife, "but carrying him wasn't the hard part. It was picking him up and putting him down after each shot that was difficult."

***

Every seat in the football stadium was sold except one. It was Grand Final day. A television reporter noticed the empty seat and thought there might be a story.

"Why is this seat empty?" he asked a man sitting beside it.

"That's my wife's seat," came the reply.

"Then why isn't she here?"

"She died last week," replied the man.

"I'm so sorry to hear that," said the reporter, "but surely you could have found a friend to come with you today."

"No," replied the man, "they're all at the funeral."

***

Jesus was relieving St Peter at the Pearly Gates. An old man asked for admission.

"Name?" said Jesus.

"Joseph."

"Occupation?"

"Carpenter."

Jesus became excited. "Did you have a son?" asked Jesus.

"Yes."

"Did he have holes in his wrists and ankles?"

"Yes!" said the old man.

Jesus looked at the old man with a tear in his eye, put his arms out and said, "Father! Father! It's me! It's me!"

The old man looked puzzled, then beamed – "Pinocchio!"

***

Private Smith's mother had died unexpectedly and the Sergeant Major had to break the news to him.

"Break it gently to him," advised his Lieutenant.

It was parade time, and the Sergeant Major was giving his troops a quick inspection.

"Brown! Straighten your hat! Jones! Your shoes are filthy. Johnson! Button up your jacket. Smith! Your mother's dead."

Smith's knees buckled, and he was carried off to Sick Bay.

A few weeks later, Private Smith's father died, and the Sergeant Major again had to pass on the bad news.

"Break it to him gently," said the Lieutenant. "You saw what happened last time."

Out on the parade ground, the Sergeant Major called his men to attention.

"All those who have a father take one step forward!" he roared. "And where do you think you're going, Private Smith?"

REAL GOERS

The dancing school barred Dave from the hokey pokey class.

He kept putting it in when you're supposed to shake it all about.

***

The cabaret dancer said her left leg was pretty good, her right was even better, and between the two she could make a fortune.

***

Phil was also banned from the dance class because of the way he did the fandango. He had his fan in one hand and his dango in the other.

***

The Rifle Club invited Jack to a small bore shooting competition. When he arrived they stood him on a box and started firing at him.

***

Did you hear about the English nymphomaniac?
   She had to have a man every six months, no matter what.

***

A Jewish nymphomaniac is one who will let her husband make love to her after she's just returned from the beauty parlour.

RED LIGHT

What do you get when you cross a computer with a prostitute?
   A fucking know-it-all.

***

What did the leper say to the prostitute?
   You can keep the tip.

***

Two young women met for a cup of coffee after being out of touch for many years. They asked each other what sort of work they were doing.

"I'm a receptionist at a hotel. I'm getting half my board," said one.

"Gee," chided the other, "I work in a massage parlour and get my hole bored."

***

A dejected used-car salesman was sitting in the corner drowning his problems.

"What's up?" asked the local harlot.

"Things aren't going too well. If I don't sell more cars, I'll lose my arse."

"I know how you feel," said the harlot. "If I don't sell more arse this month, I'll lose my car."

***

He was eight feet tall and asked the Madam if she had a girl his height.

"No," she replied. "In fact, the only two girls available are about four feet tall."

"That's O.K.," he said. "I'll screw them together."

***

A man is driving down a deserted stretch of American highway when he notices a sign out of the corner of his eye. It reads, "Sisters Of Mercy House Of Prostitution – 10 Miles".

He thinks it is just a figment of his imagination, and drives on without a second thought. Soon, he sees another sign which says, "Sisters of Mercy House Of Prostitution – 5 Miles", and realises that these signs are real.

When he drives past a third sign saying, "Sisters of Mercy House Of Prostitution – Next Right", his curiosity gets the best of him and he pulls into the driveway. On the far side of the parking lot is a sombre stone building with a small sign next to the door reading "Sisters of Mercy".

He climbs the steps and rings the bell. The door is answered by a nun in a long black habit who asks, "What may we do for you, my son?"

He answers, "I saw your signs along the highway and am very interested in doing business."

"Very well, my son. Please follow me."

He is led through many winding passages and is soon disoriented. The nun stops at a closed door and tells the man, "Please knock on this door."

He does as he is told and the door is answered by another nun in a long habit who is holding a tin cup. This nun instructs, "Please place $50 in the cup, then go through the large wooden door at the end of this hallway."

He gets $50 out of his wallet and places it in the second nun's cup. He trots eagerly down the hall and slips through the door, pulling it shut. As the door locks behind him, he finds himself back in the parking lot, facing another sign which reads, "Go In Peace. You Have Just Been Screwed By The Sisters Of Mercy."

***

What's the different between a counterfeit note and a skinny prostitute?

One's a phoney buck.

***

The prostitute was visiting her psychoanalyst. One intimate question led to another, and before he knew it, the shrink was on the couch, bonking his patient.

When it was all over, they looked at each other for a moment and then exchanged $100 bills.

***

REINCARNATION

Rex the labrador knocked a paling off the back garden fence, came back home and deposited the neighbour's now-dead rabbit at the back door. Rex's owner, Barney, was very upset, for he knew how much his neighbour's children loved the rabbit.

He decided that the best thing to do was to clean the rabbit up, put it back in its cage, and everyone would think that it died from some disease. He shampooed the rabbit in the bath, brushed off the dirt and blood and blow-dried its fur. It looked as good as new again. He carefully placed it back in the rabbit cage.

That night, Barney's neighbour came hammering on his door. Barney flew into a panic. His neighbour had found the rabbit dead. Tentatively he opened the door and saw his neighbour's stunned face.

"What's wrong?" asked Barney.

"Come and have a look at this!" replied the neighbour. He took Barney to the rabbit's cage. "This morning," said the neighbour, "I ran over the rabbit and killed it. I buried it in the garden and now it's back in its cage!"

REPARTEE

It took time, but Len eventually developed an attachment for his mother-in-law. It fitted over her mouth.

***

"You're a typical hen-pecked spineless husband!" the drinker told Bill.

"You wouldn't have the guts to say that if my missus was here!" replied Bill.

***

"I think you should know before we go too far that I am a lesbian."

"That's O.K., I've got a cousin in Beirut."

***

"Are you a virgin?"

"Yes, but I'm not a fanatic about it."

***

"How would you like a Harvey Wallbanger?"

"I'd love one, but let's have a drink first."

***

"I'm yours for the asking."

"I'm asking $50."

RESEARCH

Research proves that 22% of men like girls with big legs, 34% of men like girls with slender legs, and the rest said they liked something in between.

RESOURCEFULNESS

How can we solve the world's problems?

Get the hungry to eat the homeless.

***

Irene was stark naked when she arrived at the fancy dress ball.

"You must be dressed as something!" said the doorman.

So Irene put on a pair of black gloves, put on a pair of black shoes, and announced, "I'm the Five of Spades."

***

He was obviously trying to impress her as they walked into the jewellery shop on Friday night.

"Choose any diamond ring you'd like, darling," he said, gesturing flamboyantly.

She chose a five-carat setting worth $40,000.

"Can I pay by cheque?" he asked the manager.

"Certainly, sir, but of course you understand that we will have to keep the ring until the cheque is cleared."

A few days later, he returned to the jewellers. The concerned manager said, "I'm afraid your cheque has bounced."

"Yes, I know," he said, "I just dropped by to thank you and say that I had a really great weekend."

***

Leo went to the doctor for his annual check-up. The doctor checked his heart and blood pressure and frowned.

"You've got ten hours to live," he said.

"I demand a second opinion," said Leo, and rushed off to a heart specialist.

The heart specialist checked him out immediately and said, "Leo, you've got nine hours to live."

Leo jumped into his car and raced home to his wife.

"Darling," he said, "I have only eight hours to live."

"What do you want to do in your final hours, Leo?"

"I want to make love," said Leo.

So they jumped into bed.

During their post-coital cigarette, Leo said, "I've got seven hours to live. Can we make love again?"

"Of course," said his loving wife.

After another hour, and another post-coital cigarette, he said, "Darling, I have only six hours to live. Let's do it again."

"For Christ's sake, Leo," she said, "it's O.K. for you! You don't have to get up early in the morning."

***

The cab broke down in a lonely part of town. The driver got out and lifted the hood. His pretty young passenger called out, "Do you want a screwdriver?"

"Yes, Miss," he replied, "but wait till I've fixed the motor."

BONKS

A tortoise had been raped by two snails.

"Describe them," demanded the police.

"I can't," said the tortoise, "it happened too fast."

***

"Doctor I'm getting married tomorrow and I don't know much about men. Can I ask you a question?"

"Certainly Miss, go ahead."

"I saw my fiancé with his pants off last night and hanging between his legs he's got a great big dic ..."

"Organ, Miss! It's called an Organ!"

"Call it what you like Doc, it looks like a clarinet to me."

***

S.T.D.s

Green fungus was growing all over his balls and he anxiously rushed to the hospital to remedy the problem. A specimen was taken and investigated by the hospital scientists. Finally the report came back.

"You've heard of cauliflower ears?" said the doctor. "Well you've got brothel sprouts."

***

Patrick picked Maureen up at the local Rave Party. Later he took her home and she asked him to go to bed with her.

"I've got no protection," said Patrick.

"That's O.K.," said Maureen, "but be careful."

Patrick was just working up a full head of steam when he stopped dead and looked at her and said, "You don't have AIDS, do you?"

"No," said Maureen, "of course not!"

"That's a relief," said Patrick, "I don't want to catch it twice."

SHAGGY DOGS

A teenager in jeans, braces and Doc Marten boots was travelling on a late-night train. In the carriage with him was an old lady, an attractive young woman and a policeman.

As they entered the subway, the lights went out. In the darkness a kiss and a heavy blow could be heard. When the lights came on, the policeman was rubbing a swollen eye.

The old lady thought, "That young lady must know self-defence and she hit the policeman for his unwelcome attention."

The young woman thought, "Why would that policeman want to kiss that old lady instead of an attractive young woman like me?"

The policeman thought, "That vandal in the Doc Martens must have made advances on the young lady. In the darkness she went to punch him, missed and hit me!"

But here's what really happened. The teenager kissed the back of his own hand and punched the policeman.

***

Eric was a keen bear hunter. One day whilst out hunting he spotted a huge brown bear on the edge of a clearing. Aiming his rifle, he fired a couple of shots. He rushed to the edge of the clearing, expecting to find the dead bear. To his horror, he found the bear very much alive.

"I'm sick to death of you hunters shooting at me all the time," said the bear, "and I'm going to teach you a lesson. Get down on your knees and give me a blow job. Now!"

Eric obeyed.

The next day, Eric returned to the spot with a buffalo gun. He was going to get even with this bear. Sure enough, there was the bear on the edge of the clearing. Eric lined him up and pulled the trigger. He dashed to the edge of the clearing, expecting to see the dead bear. But again, there was the bear, waiting for him.

"You'll never learn," said the bear. "Down on your hands and knees and give me another blow job."

Eric obeyed again.

Next day, he returned with an elephant gun. He was going to get this bear for sure this time. There was the bear, standing on the edge of the clearing.

He crept closer, took aim and fired. He rushed over to the spot where the bear had been standing, and there was the bear, waiting for him.

"O.K.," said the bear, "let's have the truth – you're not in this for the hunting at all, are you?"

***

There was a fly buzzing about one foot above the river. A trout saw the fly and thought, "If that fly comes down six inches I can jump out of the water and catch it."

What the trout didn't see was a bear hiding behind a bush who also saw the fly and realised what the trout was up to and thought, "If I wait until the fly drops six inches, the trout will jump and I'll catch the trout."

There was a hunter watching the bear watching the trout watching the fly. He thought, "When the fly drops six inches and the trout jumps and the bear grabs the trout, I'll be able to shoot the bear."

It was a long wait, so the hunter munched on a cheese sandwich.

There was a mouse watching the hunter watching the bear watching the trout watching the fly. The mouse thought, "When the hunter shoots the bear he'll put down his sandwich and I'll steal the cheese."

There was a cat who was watching the mouse watching the hunter who was watching the bear who was watching the trout who was watching the fly. The cat figured that if the fly dropped six inches, the trout would jump out of the water, the bear would grab the trout, the hunter would shoot the bear, the mouse would grab the cheese and he would grab the mouse.

All of a sudden the fly dropped six inches, the trout jumped out of the water, the bear grabbed the trout, the hunter shot the bear, the mouse ran for the cheese and the cat went for the mouse .... but missed and fell into the river.

The moral of the story? When the fly drops six inches the pussy gets wet.

***

An old farmer decided it was time to get a new rooster for his hens. The rooster he had was doing a poor job and was getting old. The farmer figured a new rooster could do a better job.

So he bought a new one and turned him loose in the barnyard. The old rooster saw the young one strutting around amongst the hens and got a bit worried.

"They're trying to replace me," he thought. "I've got to do something about this."

So he walked up to the new bird and said, "So you're the new stud around here. I bet you think you're pretty good! Well, let me tell you, I'm not ready for the chopping block. And to prove it, I'll challenge you to a race around the barn. Ten times around, and whoever finishes first has all the hens to himself and the loser takes off."

The young rooster thought he was more than a match, and said, "You're on!"

The old rooster said, "I'm so great, I'll give you half a lap start and still beat you!"

So the two roosters went over to the barn and started the race. After the first lap the old rooster was gaining on the young one. After the second lap he had made up more ground, and still more after the third. But the old rooster tired and started to slip back each time round. By the eighth lap, he was just barely in front of the young rooster.

The farmer had heard all the commotion in the barnyard. He ran into the house, got his shotgun and ran out to the barn, figuring a fox was after his hens. When he got there he saw two roosters running round the barn, the old rooster still slightly in front. He immediately took aim, fired and shot the young rooster dead.

As he walked away he mumbled to himself, "I'll be damned – that's the third gay rooster I've had this month."

***

Brown Eagle had proved himself to be a very brave warrior and was now entitled to take a wife. He chose the most beautiful squaw in his village. Before the wedding he jumped on his horse and rode to the Trading Post. He said to the trader, "I am marrying the most beautiful squaw in my village. I want a very special wedding gift for her."

The trader suggested a large soft buffalo hide, and every night he rolled up in the hide with his beautiful squaw.

Brown Eagle became the most heroic warrior of his Indian tribe and was able to take another wife. He chose the most beautiful squaw of his whole tribe. Again he hopped on his horse and rode to the Trading Post, telling the trader, "I am marrying the most beautiful squaw of my whole tribe. I want a very special wedding gift for her."

The trader suggested a beautiful bear hide that would keep her very warm on the cold winter nights.

Brown Eagle went on to become the Chief of the whole Indian nation and could now take a third wife. He chose the most beautiful squaw in the whole Indian nation and again, jumped on his horse, galloped to the Trading Post and said to the trader, "I am now a big Chief. I am marrying the most beautiful squaw in the whole of the Indian nation. I want a very special wedding gift for her."

The trader said, "I have on my shelf a hippopotamus hide. It's the only hide like it in the country. It is thick, soft leather. It's huge. It will never wear out. Your squaw can wrap herself in it in the long winter nights and never be cold."

Brown Eagle decided that it was time to settle down and raise a family. His three squaws got pregnant at the same time. When they gave birth, the squaw on the buffalo hide had a baby girl, while the squaw on the bear hide had a baby boy, but the squaw on the hippopotamus hide had twins – a boy and a girl. This proves that:

The Squaw on the Hippopotamus is Equal to the Sum of the Squaws on the other Two Hides.

***

A man was lost bush-walking. It was getting dark and it was raining. He had nowhere to stay so he ran up to a farmhouse and knocked on the door.

"Can you please give me a room for the night?" he asked the woman owner.

"Yes, you can sleep in the barn," she said sympathetically.

The man walked to the barn in the dark and got tangled in the clothes line, tearing some clothes and dropping others on the ground.

He sat down in the barn and began to shave. There was a loud thunder clap and the man dropped his razor. It landed on the cat and shaved some cat hair off. The cat jumped up, giving the man a fright and he fell backwards hitting a shelf of paints. The paints fell onto a donkey and the donkey squealed.

The woman came running.

"I'm calling the cops," she yelled, picking up the phone.

"Hello Officer?" she said. "A man just ran into my house, ripped off my clothes, shaved my pussy and painted my ass!"

***

Texas is the biggest State of North America and Texans reckon they have the biggest of everything. There was a Texan girl who met a Texan cowboy in the world's biggest bar in Texas.

He bragged, "I've got the biggest feet in the world, size 20."

She went one better, "I've got the biggest cunt in the world."

"I'd have to see that," said the cowboy, so they went around to his motel. He took his size 20 boots off and said, "I'll bet you can't even get the big toe of one of these up there."

She just smiled and said, "Try me, cowboy."

She spread her legs high in the air and the Texan slid the whole boot in and said, "Wow!"

He then took his other boot and slid the whole boot in.

She said, "I didn't even feel that, cowboy."

So the cowboy said, "I must have a look at this," bent over and stuck his whole head in. Before he knew it, he tripped over the carpet and fell right inside.

Groping around, he brought out his flashlight and, to his amazement, saw another guy in there.

"What are you doing here?" the cowboy asked.

"Same thing as you," was the reply.

"Well, it's a good thing I've got this flashlight so we can find our way out of here," the cowboy said.

But the other guy replied, "Let's use it to look around first. If we can find my horse, we can ride out of here."

***

Maureen had her eye on Cameron for a long time. But Cameron was oblivious to her romantic overtures. He was obsessed with his Harley motor cycle, for which he had a deep passion.

One day he was lubricating his bike with Vaseline when Maureen called in and asked if he would like to come to tea on Saturday night.

"Can I bring my bike?" Cameron asked.

"I guess so," said Maureen.

On Saturday night, Cameron turned up on his Harley, the tank and the chromework sparkling.

"Can I bring my bike inside?" he asked Maureen's mother.

"No, leave it on the porch," Mother said.

"All right," said Cameron, "but if it's staying out here in the moist air, I need to give it another rub of Vaseline to keep the rust away. I do this every night," he said, pulling out the jar and a cloth.

It was a most enjoyable meal and as everyone was about to leave the table, Maureen's mother said, "Hold on a bit, where are you all going? I'm not going to wash the dishes."

"Well, I'm not," said Maureen.

"And I'm not," said Maureen's father.

"And I'm certainly not," said Cameron. "It looks like rain and I want to polish my bike."

"Well," said Mother, "I cooked the meal and I'm not doing the dishes."

"Enough!" roared Father. "No more arguments. Not another word. In fact, whoever says the next word will do the dishes!"

They all sat there in silence. Outside there was a flash

of lightning and a roll of thunder, and Cameron was becoming most anxious about the possible rain on his bike. He desperately wanted the jar of Vaseline to rub over the frame and the tank, but silence persisted.

Another clap of thunder, and Cameron decided that he would force somebody else to speak. He got up, pushed Maureen to the floor, tore off her clothes and had his way with her. Mother and Father were horrified, but not a word was spoken.

Cameron decided his actions must be more drastic. He jumped on Mother, threw her to the floor and had his way with her too.

Father gritted his teeth, but not a word passed his lips.

What else could Cameron do? He was defeated. As he heard the rain falling on the roof, he got up from the table and said, "O.K., I'm going to get the Vaseline."

"I'll do the dishes! I'll do the dishes!" yelled Father, jumping up and dashing into the kitchen.

***

Quasimodo, the Hunchback of Notre Dame, had a unique way of ringing the church bells. He would stand on the parapet, calculate the wind speed, swing off towards the bell and kick it with his feet.

Unfortunately for Quasi, he misjudged the wind one stormy day, twisted in mid air, hit the bell with his head and fell to the ground, dead. A crowd quickly gathered and a policeman was called.

"Does anybody know this man?" the policeman asked of the crowd.

One man came forward, looked at Quasi and said, "No, but his face rings a bell."

***

Quasimodo's twin brother was hired to replace Quasi after he died. Quasi had taught him how to swing on the rope and kick the bell with his feet. The brother misjudged the wind one day also and fell dead on the pavement.

A crowd quickly gathered and a policeman was called.

"Can anyone identify this man?" asked the policeman of the crowd.

"Yes," said someone, "he's a dead ringer for his brother."

***

One sunny Sunday, Superman was flying around with nothing to do, so he decided to drop in on Batman.

"Hi, Bat," said Superman, "let's go down the pub and have a beer."

"Not today, Super. My Batmobile's broken down and I've got to fix it. Can't fight crime without it, you know."

Disappointed, Superman went over to Spiderman's place.

"Let's go down the pub for a drink, Spider."

"Sorry Super. I've got a problem with my web gun. Can't fight crime without it, you know."

Dejectedly, Superman took to the air again, and decided to drop by on Wonder Woman. There she was, lying on her back out on her balcony, stark naked and writhing around. Superman conceived a cunning idea. "Everyone says I'm faster than a speeding bullet, and I've always wondered what sort of screw she'd be."

So he zoomed down, did her in a flash and zoomed off.

"What the hell was that!" cried Wonder Woman.

"I don't know, but it hurt like hell!" said the Invisible Man.

***

St Peter was doing market research with the applicants at the Pearly Gates. Three men were awaiting entry.

"Cause of death?" St Peter asked the first.

"I suspected my wife was cheating on me," the first man replied, "so I came home early and burst into my apartment on the twenty-first floor. I ran into the bedroom and my wife was lying naked on the bed. I searched the apartment but found no-one. I went out on the balcony, and sure enough, there was a man hanging by his fingers. I went inside and got a hammer and started beating his fingers. He let go and fell, but hit the awning across the pavement. I could see that he was still alive, so I rushed back into the apartment, grabbed the refrigerator, pushed it over the balcony and let it fall. The effort was too much for me and I had a heart attack and fell down dead."

"Next?" said St Peter. "Cause of death?"

"I lived on the twenty-second floor of an apartment building. I always do my exercises out on the balcony and today I fell, but I was lucky. I grabbed hold of the railing on the balcony below, when suddenly, this guy came out and started beating my fingers with a hammer. I had to let go, but I dropped onto an awning beneath. Next thing, a refrigerator dropped out of the sky and crushed me. That's why I'm here."

"Next?" said St Peter. "Cause of death?"

"Well ... I was hiding in this refrigerator ....."

***

Jesus, nailed to the cross, sees Peter in the crowd.

"Peter," he calls, "Peter."

Peter hears his name and calls, "I hear you, My Lord. I'm coming."

Peter begins to walk up the hill to the cross but is challenged by a Roman Centurion.

"Stop!" said the Centurion. "Or I'll cut off your arm."

"But I must go. My Lord is calling."

The Centurion swung his sword and severed Peter's arm.

"Peter, Peter," called Jesus.

Peter staggered up the hill, only to be confronted by another Centurion.

"Stop! Or I will cut off your other arm," said the Centurion.

"But I must continue. My Lord is calling me."

The Centurion swung his sword and cut off Peter's other arm.

Peter staggered on up the hill, becoming weak from loss of blood and still he heard Jesus calling, "Peter, Peter."

Again, he was confronted by a Centurion.

"Stop! Or I'll cut off your leg!"

"But My Lord is calling me," replied Peter, as he attempted to climb the hill. The Centurion swung his mighty sword and cut off Peter's leg.

"Peter, Peter," called Jesus.

In great pain, Peter began to hop up the hill, and as he neared the bottom of the cross, he was confronted by yet another Centurion who said, "Stop, or I will cut off your other leg."

"Peter, Peter," cried Jesus.

"Can't you hear? My Lord is calling me."

"I don't care," said the Centurion, and cut off Peter's other leg.

Peter dragged his mutilated body to the bottom of the cross, his eyes focused on Jesus. "I am here, Lord. I have answered your call."

Jesus looked down at Peter and said, "Peter ... I can see your house from up here!"

SHOPPING SPREES

A woman walked into a sex shop and asked to buy a vibrator. The shop assistant beckoned with his finger and said, "Can you come this way."

The woman replied, "If I could come that way, I wouldn't need a vibrator."

***

She was gazing in the window of the shoe shop, admiring a beautiful pair of black Italian stiletto-heeled shoes, priced far beyond her capacity to pay.

The shoe salesman in the shop beckoned her in. "You can have those shoes if you come to bed with me," he said.

"O.K.," she replied, "but I should tell you, I don't like sex very much."

He gave her the shoes and they booked into a motel room. They took off their clothes and jumped into bed. He humped away while she lay passively, missionary style. Suddenly, she threw her legs up into the air and cried, "Wonderful! ..... Beautiful! ..... Oh my God, so lovely! ......"

"I thought you didn't like sex," he panted.

"I don't," she replied, "I'm just admiring my beautiful new shoes."

***

Diana and Barbara were in the shopping centre.

"There's my husband, coming out of the florist with a dozen roses. That means I'm going to have to keep my legs up in the air for three days," said Diana.

"Why?" said Barbara. "Don't you have a vase?"

***

Pete had an embarrassing twitch in his eye. He had tried everything to get rid of it. At last he found a Chinese doctor who told him that a regular dose of aspirin would fix his problem.

When he returned, Dr Woo asked him how he was progressing.

"No good," said Peter. "Every time I go into the drug store and ask for a packet of aspirin, they give me these!", and he threw down fifty packets of condoms.

***

A blind man went into a department store, picked up his guide dog by the tail and began swinging him around.

A sales clerk came over and said, "Can I be of assistance?"

"No," said the blind man, "I'm just looking around."

SHRINKS

The pressure was too much for the Stock Exchange executive. He had a breakdown and was committed to a mental hospital. During therapy time, he said he was having sex with biscuits.

"Are they chocolate biscuits?"

"No," he said.

"Are they shortbreads?"

"No."

"Are they those dry biscuits with pepper and salt on them?"

"Yes, yes, that's the sort!"

"Then you're fuckin' crackers!"

***

The blonde patient pleaded with her psychiatrist. "Kiss me! Please, kiss me!"

"No," said the psychiatrist, "that's unethical, Miss. I shouldn't even be screwing you."

***

"Doctor, doctor, can you help me? I'm suffering from a premature ejaculation problem."

"I can't cure you of your problem," said the doctor, "but I can put you in touch with a woman who has a short attention span."

***

A beautiful young thing goes to see a psychotherapist.

"Take off your clothes and lie on the couch," he instructed.

He then jumped on the couch with her and ravished her.

When he finished, he put his clothes on and said, "Well, that's my problem solved – what's yours?"

***

A soldier was having a psychiatric test prior to discharge. The psychiatrist asked, "Tell me, Private, what would happen if I cut off one of your ears?"

"It would be hard to hear," replied the soldier.

"Good," said the psychiatrist. "What would happen if I cut off your other ear?"

"I wouldn't be able to see."

"That's interesting, why do you say that?"

"Because my cap would fall over my eyes."

***

A public speaker had an appointment with his psychiatrist who ran his private practice at a mental hospital. Whilst in the waiting room, the psychiatrist came out and said, "You're a public speaker, aren't you? Would you do me a favour? I've got a group of hospital patients in the lecture room and the speaker hasn't turned up. Could you fill in for an hour or so?"

"Certainly," said the public speaker.

The speaker stood behind the lectern and looked down at the group of patients, who stared blankly at him. But being a pro, he gave forth his most motivational talk. He was constantly being interrupted, however, by a patient at the back of the room, who kept calling out, "Bullshit."

When he had finished speaking, the speaker said to his psychiatrist that he didn't think the man at the back of the room was very impressed with his motivational talk.

"No!" said the psychiatrist. "You were fantastic! That's the first intelligent thing that patient has said in three years!"

***

"**D**octor, I keep thinking I'm a wheelbarrow."

"Well, you must stop people pushing you around."

***

A young man went to the psychiatrist complaining that he was getting married and he was worried about the small size of his penis. The psychiatrist advised him to go and stay on a dairy farm, and every morning, dip his penis in milk and get it sucked by a calf.

Some time later, the young man met the psychiatrist in the street.

"How's the marriage going?" asked the psychiatrist.

"I never got married," said the young man. "I cancelled it and bought the calf."

***

Garry was depressed, he told his psychiatrist, because he thought he was gay.

"Why do you feel that way?"

"Because my father was a gay."

"Being a poof is not hereditary," said the psychiatrist.

"My brother is gay."

"That still doesn't mean that you are."

"My Uncle Bruce is gay. And my cousin Jeffrey is gay."

The psychiatrist gave a concerned look and frowned.

"Does anyone in your family have sexual contact with women?" he asked.

"Yes," said Garry, "my sister does."

***

It was the end of the football season and many football fans were suffering from withdrawal symptoms. One psychiatrist had a thriving business helping them get through it.

One day he had a patient on the couch and he said to him, "Imagine something brown, firm, with smooth curves."

The patient thought for a moment and said, "A football."

"Good," said the psychiatrist. "What do you think of when two arms slide around your waist?"

"A tackle."

"Good," he said. "Now picture a pair of firm thighs."

"A half-back!" came the reply.

"Your reactions are quite normal," said the psychiatrist. "You'd be surprised at some of the stupid answers I get."

***

"I've got to change jobs," the patient said to his psychiatrist. "I've worked in a pickled onion factory for ten years, and last week I started to get this uncontrollable urge to put my dick in the onion peeler."

The psychiatrist explained about workplace stress and told him he must learn to relax.

But a week later, the patient was back.

"I don't think I can control myself much longer," he said. "The urge is getting greater. I'm going to put my dick in the onion peeler any day now."

The psychiatrist prescribed Valium.

A month later, the patient was back on the psychiatrist's couch.

"I've lost my job," he said. "I finally stuck my dick into the onion peeler."

"My God!" said the psychiatrist. "What happened then?"

"I got fired. And Betty, the onion peeler, got fired too."

***

SINGLES BARS

Zeke was only in town for one night so he headed for the singles bar for a quick pick-up. He approached the first woman he saw.

"I'm only in town for one night," he said, "and I can't waste time. Do you fuck or don't you?"

"Well," she replied coyly, "I don't usually, but you've sweet-talked me into it."

***

A guy meets a girl in the bar and she goes home with him. When they are relaxing after making love, he asks, "Am I the first guy you ever made love to?"

She looks at him for a few moments and says, "Of course you are! Why do you men always ask that same stupid question?"

***

Max was desperate for some female company. He started a conversation with a blonde in the corner who accepted his invitation to an expensive hotel restaurant. She had two servings of every course, thoroughly enjoying her outing.

"Do you always eat this much?" asked Max, thinking about the cost.

"Only when I've got a heavy period," replied the blonde.

***

They had just met that night and were having a post-coital conversation.

"If I get pregnant," she said, "what will we call the baby?"

Pulling off his condom, tying it in a knot and flushing it down the toilet, he said, "Well, if he gets out of that, we'll call him Houdini."

***

After a few drinks and small talk, she invited him back to her apartment. Just before they turned out the light, he asked, "How do you like your eggs in the morning?"

"Unfertilised," she replied.

***

"How about a screw?" he asked.

"Your place or mine?" she replied.

"If you're going to argue, forget it!" he said.

***

She was sitting at the bar with a lonely look on her face. He sidled up to her and whispered in her ear, "What would you say if I stole a kiss?"

"The same thing I'd say to any dickhead who had the chance to steal a car but only took the hubcaps!" she said.

***

He was driving her home after an enjoyable night at the Singles Disco. He pulled into a shady lane and started to grope her.

"Do you know what good clean fun is?" she said, pushing his hand away.

"No," he replied, "what good is it?"

***

When she met him in the Singles Bar, she told him she was a Libra on the cusp of Scorpio. He replied that he was Taurus with penis rising.

***

It was her first night at the Singles Bar and the handsome young guy had asked her home to watch some videos.

"No funny business? Nothing serious?" she asked.

"Trust me. We'll just watch a few movies."

"But what if I've seen the movies?"

"Well, you can put your clothes on and go home."

SPORTING HEROES

Ossie approached the umpire after a series of bad decisions.

"If I called you a stupid bastard who didn't know the first thing about the rules of football, what would you do?" he said.

"I'd report you and you'd be fined," replied the umpire.

"What if I didn't say it and I just thought it?" said Ossie.

"Well, there's nothing I can do about that."

"O.K.," said Ossie, "we'll just leave it at that."

***

A young footballer was shipwrecked on a tropical island with Miss Universe. He couldn't believe his luck, but she was prim and proper.

"You live on one side of the island, and I'll live on the other," she said, "and we'll meet once a week to discuss any rescue prospects."

This went on for a month, and when they next met, they were both as horny as hell.

"We might as well do it," he said, "we could spend the rest of our lives here."

"I agree," she said, and tore her clothes off. They screwed for hours.

"Let's meet again tomorrow," said Miss Universe.

"Could you do me a favour?" said the football player.

"Sure," she said.

"I've got some shirts and trousers here." he said. "Could you dress up as a man?"

She reluctantly consented, thinking he was a bit kinky.

Next day as she walked up the beach dressed like a man the footballer walked up beside her.

"G'day mate," he said, slapping her on the back, "you'll never guess who I fucked last night."

***

The crew from the winning boat were lined up on the dais to receive their gold medal when a blonde rushed out of the crowd and kissed their cox.

STAR GAZERS

The Hollywood talent scout had just heard a young man give a very funny and live performance.

"That was great!" he said. "What's your name?"

"Penis van Lesbian," said the young comedian.

"Wow! We'll have to change that. How about we call you Dick Van Dyke?"

***

During the first quarter of the next New Moon, go outside at 11 p.m. and face the South. Bend over at the waist to form a ninety-degree angle. Bend the knees at a forty-five-degree angle. Then, get a hand mirror and hold it between your legs. With a bit of luck, if all the angles are correct, you should see Uranus.

THE DIFFERENCE IS ...

What do you get when you cross a disobedient dog with a rooster?
You get a cock that won't come.

***

Why is American beer like making love in a boat?
They're both fucking near water.

***

What's the difference between a woman in a singles bar and a proctologist?
The proctologist only has to deal with one arsehole at a time.

***

What's got 3 balls and flies through space?
The Extra Testicle.

***

What's the difference between Jurassic Park and I.B.M.?

One is a high-tech theme park dominated by dinosaurs. The other is a Steven Spielberg film.

***

What's the different between erotic and kinky?
Erotic is when you use a feather.
Kinky is when you use the whole chicken.

***

What's the difference between a vitamin and a hormone?
You can't hear a vitamin.

***

What's the difference between a slut and a bitch?
A slut will sleep with anyone.
A bitch will sleep with anyone but you.

TOURISTS

Two Australians in London who were down on their luck saw an advertisement for two footmen at Buckingham Palace. "References essential", it said. "That's O.K.," said Col, "we can write them out for each other."

They arrived at the Palace and offered the Queen two glowing references. "Our servants dress in formal Scottish attire. This means wearing kilts, so drop your trousers while I check your knees."

The Aussies were a little surprised, but they did so. The Queen gave the knees a nod of approval and said, "Okay, now let me see those testimonials."

After they were thrown out of the Palace, Col said, "Y'know, if we'd understood the local lingo, I reckon we could've got those jobs."

***

The two women were side by side in their deckchairs on the Q.E.2 enjoying a round-the-world cruise. The first one said, "My husband worked hard all his life so we could have a trip like this."

The other woman looked at her and said haughtily, "Oh, your first trip, is it? I have had fifteen trips like this. My husband works for Cunard."

"Well!" said the first. "My husband works fuckin' hard too, but I don't swear about it!"

***

Bill had just returned home from a sales convention in Hong Kong. He spent his days at the convention and his nights in the Red Light district, and was now suffering from a painful and inflamed penis. He hurried to the doctor, who diagnosed it as the Hong Kong Dong and told Bill he would have to have his penis amputated.

Bill was shocked and sought a second opinion, only to be given the same advice – amputation.

A friend recommended a Chinese doctor who practised traditional medicine. The Chinese doctor confirmed the Hong Kong Dong diagnosis but said there was no need for amputation.

"I'm so relieved!" said Bill.

"Yes," said the Chinese medico, "in a week's time it will drop off by itself."

***

Bob had just returned from Hong Kong and the doctor had diagnosed the Hong Kong Dong.

"I'm afraid it's got to come off," he said.

Bob was horrified.

"Don't worry," said the doctor. "You can have a transplant."

"How much would that cost?" asked Bob.

"$500 for a standard model, $1,000 for a big one and $2,000 for a big black one," replied the doctor.

"I'll have to talk this over with my wife," responded Bob.

Bob returned to the doctor the next day.

"Don't worry about the transplant, doc. We've decided to get a new kitchen instead," he said.

***

A man in a Japanese restaurant calls to the waiter, "This chicken is rubbery!"

The waiter smiled and said, "Ah, thank you very much!"

***

The young tourist was exploring the Red Light district of Bangkok and thought he would try one of the well-known Parlours.

"Sorry," said the Madam, "there are no girls available tonight."

Disappointed, he turned to leave.

"Wait!" said the Madam, "we do have a beautiful young female pig available, and she's very popular with many of our clients. I can guarantee you'll enjoy it."

"Why not!" he thought.

He paid his money and had his way with the pig.

It was so enjoyable that he was back at the same Parlour the next night, asking for the pig.

"I'm sorry," said the Madam, "the pig's not available, but there's a good show on tonight – a donkey with one of our girls."

He paid his money and took his seat behind the two-way mirror.

"Gee," he said to the man sitting next to him, "this is incredible."

"It's nothing," said the stranger. "You should have been here last night. There was a man fucking a pig."

VEGETARIAN

"I heard you married again."

"Yes, for the fourth time."

"What happened to the first three?"

"They all died."

"What happened?"

"My first wife ate poison mushrooms."

"How sad. What happened to your second wife?"

"She ate poison mushrooms too."

"What about the third wife. Did she eat poison mushrooms?"

"No, she died of a broken neck."

"Had an accident, eh?"

"No. She wouldn't eat her mushrooms."

VIVE LA FRANCE

An Australian, an Englishman and a Frenchman were discussing the meaning of 'savoir faire'. The Australian gave an example:

"Say a man comes home and finds his best mate screwing his wife in bed. He says, 'G'day Shirley, g'day George. Never mind me, just carry on. I'll go and get a beer.' That's savoir faire!"

The Englishman said, "By jove, that's a good one, but we'd do it a little differently. A chap comes home and

240

finds his chum in bed with his wife and says, 'Good evening, Shirley, good evening George, old chap. Never mind me, just carry on whilst I make a gin and tonic.' Now that's savoir faire!"

The Frenchman said, "Non! Non! Zee Frenchman comes home and finds 'is best friend in bed making zee passionate love to his wife, he says, 'Bonjour mon ami, bonjour Shirlee. Never mind me, just carry on while I pour a glass of champagne.' And my friend *continues* to make love to my wife, that's *savour faire!*"

***

Several young French boys were called by the Paris Authorities for a medical check-up to determine the father of a teenage girl's baby.

Pierre was first in, and after a few minutes came out and said, "Don't worry, they'll never find out 'oo it was. They're taking samples from the finger."

***

What's the difference between a French girl and a bowling ball?

You can only get three fingers in a bowling ball.

***

The French couple asked their ten-year-old son what he wanted for Christmas.

"I wanna watch," he replied.

So they let him.

***

A Jew, an Indian and a Frenchman were travelling across Texas when their car broke down. They knocked on a farmer's door and asked for accommodation for the night.

"I can only put up two," said the farmer, "one will have to sleep in the barn."

"I will sleep in the barn," said the Jew.

Five minutes later there was a knock on the door. "There's a pig in the barn," said the Jew, "I cannot sleep with a pig."

"O.K., I'll go," said the Indian.

Five minutes later, there was a knock on the door. "There's a cow in the barn," said the Indian, "I am a Hindu, I cannot sleep with a cow."

"I'll go," said the Frenchman.

Five minutes later, there was another knock on the door. It was the pig and the cow.

***

A Frenchman was on holidays in Australia and, while taking a drive in the countryside, saw a young child being chased by a raging bull. The Frenchman slammed on his brakes, jumped out of the car, vaulted a high fence and sprinted with amazing speed towards the bull.

Unknown to him, an Australian journalist was passing, and noticed his incredible feat. The Frenchman reached the bull and held it by the horns just five metres from the child. He flipped the bull over onto its back, twisted its head and broke its neck. He picked the child up and comforted him and carried him gently back to the side of the road.

The Australian journalist was astounded. He ran over to the Frenchman and said, "Shit-a-brick! That was incredible mate! I've never seen a man so athletic, with such strength and courage! It makes me proud to be an Australian. I'm going to put this story on the front page of every newspaper! Just give me some details about yourself. Born around here, were you?"

Next day the headlines appeared on the front page: "FRENCH PAEDOPHILE KILLS CHILD'S PET".

***

Jean Paul was so exhausted after his marriage to Suzette that when he got to the honeymoon suite he went to sleep the moment his feet hit the pillow.

***

"Take your glasses off, Pierre," Fifi demanded. "They are tearing my stockings."

Pierre did as he was commanded.

"You'd better put them back on again," she said a few minutes later. "You're licking the carpet."

***

Marcel was caught screwing his boss's fiancee. The boss sent a letter challenging Marcel to a duel.

Marcel replied in writing: "I have received your circular letter and will be present at the gathering."

WANKERS

He's so conceited that when he masturbates, he calls out his own name when he comes.

***

He fakes orgasm when he masturbates.

***

"Wake up Paula!" Peter yelled at 2am. "You won't believe what just happened! I went to have a leak and a strange light came on from nowhere. When I finished the light went out again. It's a miracle!"

"No, it's not," said Paula. "You've pissed in the bloody fridge again!"

***

What's a Yankee?

Same as a quickie except you do it alone.

***

The football coach went berserk. His team were in the middle of the ground, their shorts and jock straps round their ankles, and wanking themselves.

"What the hell are you doing?" he demanded.

"Well," said the captain, "you told us to get out here and pull ourselves together."

***

The sex expert was being interviewed. "Our research proves that half the population sing in the shower and the other half masturbate. Do you know what the singers sing?"

"No," replied the interviewer.

"I didn't think you did."

***

What's the ultimate rejection?

When your hand falls asleep while you're masturbating.

***

What's the difference between an omelette and a wank?
You can beat an omelette, but you can't beat a wank.

***

Fortunately the penis is one of the few things still exempt from taxation. The reason is because it's usually hanging around unemployed. The rest of the time, it's either hard up, pissed off or in a hole. It also has two dependants and they're both nuts and its best friend is a cunt.

***

The young parents used code words when discussing sex in front of their children. The term for intercourse was "washing machine".

They were lying in bed one night when he said to her, "Darling, washing machine."

"Not now, I've got a headache," she replied.

An hour later, he ran his hand down her leg and said, "Darling, washing machine, please! Washing machine."

"I've got a headache!" she complained.

An hour later, feeling sorry for him, she turned to him and said, "O.K., washing machine."

"Don't worry," he replied, "it was a small load so I did it by hand."

***

What is the difference between a wanker and a banker?
A wanker knows what he's doing.

***

"Doctor, I feel weak and faint."

"How many times do you have sex?" asked the doctor.

"Five or six times a night."

"Obviously that's the cause of your problem," said the doctor.

"What a relief, doc. I was afraid it might be the masturbation."

UNHAPPY MARRIAGE

"I'm divorcing my wife," Peter told his mates at the pub. "She has disgusting habits. I went to piss in the sink this morning, and it was still full of dirty dishes!"

***

Marriage has its good side. It teaches you loyalty, forbearance, tolerance, self-restraint, and other valuable qualities you wouldn't need if you'd stayed single.

***

A man came home to find his wife in bed with his friend.

"What's going on here?" demanded the husband.

"See," said the wife to her lover, "I told you he was stupid."

***

A music lover married a woman because he was infatuated by her voice. He didn't realise how ugly she was until the first morning of the honeymoon when he sat in bed and saw her without her make-up.

He stared at her for a while, then shook her and yelled: "Sing ya bitch, sing!"

***

A man died and his wife put a death notice in the paper, saying that he died of gonorrhoea. His brother phoned and complained angrily saying, "You know very well that he died of diarrhoea, not gonorrhoea."

"I know he died of diarrhoea," she replied, "but I want people to remember him as a great lover rather than the big shit he really was."

***

Bob likes to run their wedding video backwards so he can watch himself walk out of the church, a free man.

***

The husband comes home early from work and finds his neighbour in bed with his wife.

"I've looked after you all these years, you bastard!" he shouted at his neighbour, "I've lent you money, loaned you my car, after all I've done for you ... and stop doing that while I'm talking to you!"

***

Valerie had just found out that her wealthy husband Roy was having an affair with another woman.

"It's not that I don't love you," said Roy. "It's just that this other woman is so passionate. When we make love, she low moans and groans, while you just lie there and don't show any emotion."

Valerie thought about the possibility of losing Roy's

fortune, and decided to work on improving their sex life. She bought new perfume and sexy underwear and seduced Roy into bed. When Roy was screwing away, she remembered Roy's mistress's speciality of low moaning while they were having sex.

"Oh Roy, what a day I've had today," moaned Valerie. "First the washing machine broke down, then I was short-changed at the supermarket, the bus was late ..."

***

What are the three words you don't want to hear while making love?

"Darling, I'm home."

***

Advice for the man who wants excitement in his sex life:

Try "Rodeo Screwing". Mount your wife from behind and whisper, "This is how I do it with your sister", and try to stay on for eight seconds.

***

Fred had been grinding away for thirty minutes.

"What's wrong, why are you taking so long?" his wife demanded.

"I'm trying," said Fred, "but I just can't think of anyone."

***

Their love life was getting a bit boring.

"Let's do something exciting," he said, "let's do it back to back."

"That sounds great!" she said. "How do we do that?"

"We invite another couple," he replied.

***

Adam was lonely in the garden of Eden so he spoke to God.

"Hey God, how about some company?"

"OK," said God, "I'll send you Woman. She'll be beautiful, charming and intelligent. She'll cook and clean for you and she'll never argue."

"Sounds great!" said Adam. "But how much will she cost?"

"An arm and a leg, Adam."

"Gee ... what can I get for just a rib?"

***

Two friends were discussing their sex life.

"Our sex life has become boring," said one. "There doesn't seem to be any interest there any more. We don't worry about it much now. In fact, I haven't had a good screw for six months."

"Well," said the other, "it's up to you. You've got to make things interesting. I buy my wife a box of chocolates and a bunch of flowers. We sip a glass of champagne on the rug in front of the fire. Then I rip off her underclothes and screw her right there on the lounge floor. You should try that."

Next time they met, the friend asked, "Did you take my advice?"

"I sure did. Sex is fantastic now, and I just love that bear-skin rug on your lounge room floor."

***

Never forget that your wife is a romantic. She still enjoys wine, flowers and chocolate. Let her know that you, too, remember these things, by speaking of them occasionally.

***

How many men does it take to change a toilet roll?
We don't know 'cos it's never happened.

***

"I want a divorce," she told her solicitor.
"On what grounds?"
"Bigamy. He can't have his Kate and Edith too."

***

Ivan looked worried. He was explaining to his friend about his experience after the party the night before.

"I was so pissed," he said, "I can hardly remember a thing. All I know is that I woke up on top of this woman. I didn't know what to do, so I gave her $20, rolled over and went to sleep. When I woke up this morning, I was at home in bed and I realised it was my wife that I'd given the $20 to."

"Well, what's the problem?" said his friend.

"She gave me $10 change," Ivan replied.

***

Dave watched his flat-chested wife try on her new bra.

"What do you want a bra for? You've got nothing to put in them," he smirked.

"I don't complain when you buy underpants," she replied.

***

Revenge is what you feel when you seduce your enemy's wife, but sweet revenge is when you find out that she's a lousy lay.

***

George wasn't feeling too good. He felt worn out.

"How's your sex life?" asked the doctor.

"Every Saturday, Sunday, Tuesday and Thursday, never fail," said George.

"Why not cut out Sunday?" suggested the doctor.

"I can't do that. It's the only day I'm home."

***

Why does the bride always smile when she walks down the aisle?

Because she knows she'll never have to give another blow job again.

WHAT'S IN A NAME?

The Indian brave asked his father why the people of his tribe had such unusual names like Running Bear, White Eagle, Red Fox and Flying Cloud.

"We Indians name our children after first thing we see after conception.Why do you ask these questions, Broken Rubber?"

***

What do you call a woman who can suck a golf ball up a garden hose?

"Darling."

***

A young man got onto a bus and took a seat beside a most beautiful redhead.

"Hi," he said as he sat down.

"Hello," she replied. "It's a nice day, isn't it? I saw my psychiatrist today and he said that I had a problem."

"What sort of problem?" asked the young man.

"I can't tell you," replied the beautiful young thing. "I don't even know you."

"Well, sometimes it's good to talk over your problems with a perfect stranger," he replied.

"Well," she said, "my psychiatrist said that I'm a nymphomaniac who only likes to have sex with Jewish cowboys. By the way, my name's Shirley."

"Pleased to meet you, Shirley," replied the young man. "My name's Hopalong Goldberg."

WHITE COLLAR CRIME

"Oh no, it's my husband!", she said to her boyfriend on hearing the front door slam. "Quick, hide in the wardrobe!"

He grabbed his clothes and dashed from the bed to the wardrobe. After a few minutes, another voice said quietly, "It's damn dark in here, isn't it?"

The man, shivering in the nude, said, "Who's there?"

The little voice replied, "Give me $50 and I won't yell out to Dad and tell him who you are."

In no position to argue, he handed over the money, and at the appropriate time made a quick dash out the window.

The following week, Junior came home with a brand new set of roller blades. His mother queried, "Where did you get the money for those?"

"I had $50," he replied.

"Where did you get that kind of money?" but Junior wasn't telling.

Convinced her son was up to no good, she ordered him to go to church. "Confession will fix you up, my boy. You'll have to tell the priest," and she pushed him into the confessional box and shut the door.

"It's damn dark in here," he said out loud.

"Now, don't start that again!" said the priest.

***

What do you get when you cross a nun with an apple?

A computer that will never go down on you.

***

The local priest was asked to give some sex education lessons to three young nuns. He dropped his trousers and, pointing to his male appendage, asked, "Do you know what this is?"

"That's your cock," said the first nun.

"You brazen hussy! Go and rinse your mouth out with soap and water!" said the priest.

Fuming, he asked the second nun if she knew what it was.

"That's your prick," she replied.

"Get out of here, you disgusting little tramp! Scrub your mouth out with soap and water."

When he asked the third if she knew what it was, she replied, "I have no idea."

"Oh, you wonderful, innocent child," he said. "This is my penis."

She responded, "You call THAT a penis? A penis is long, thick and black!"

***

The old lady had purchased a pair of white cockatoos for company. She wanted to name them Joey and Polly but she was unable to identify which was male and which was female, so she enquired at the pet shop.

The pet shop proprietor told her to watch them and she would be able to identify the male when they were mating.

The old lady watched and waited. One day, she heard squawks and saw feathers flying and she was easily able to identify Joey. So that she would always be able to identify him, she put a white band around his neck.

Some time later, the old lady gave an afternoon tea party for the church. Joey spotted the vicar and flew onto his shoulder and squawked, "So they've caught you fuckin' round too, eh?"

***

The parish priest felt that the church was not turning out young priests in the same mould as they did in the past. His new curate was a really sharp dresser and he'd turned up in his B.M.W. sports car.

The new curate had only been around for a couple of days when he asked his senior to find him $30.

"And what would you be wanting that for?" enquired the Father.

"A nookie," replied the curate.

This puzzled the old priest. He didn't know what a nookie was, but he handed over the money.

The next day, when the priest was visiting the convent, he asked the Mother Superior, "What's a nookie?"

"$30," she replied.

***

An American advertising firm was doing research in Italy for an export sex product. A researcher approached an Italian gentleman in a black suit.

"Would you take part in a survey?" asked the researcher.

"Certainly," said the gentleman.

"How many times do you have sex, sir?"

"About six times a year," replied the man.

"What!" said the amazed researcher. "I thought Italians were supposed to be the greatest lovers on earth."

"Well," came the reply, "I'm not doing too badly for a sixty-five-year-old priest without a car."

***

Bishop O'Riordan had just completed an inspection of the prison to check out the conditions. He told the governor how delighted he was to hear that a social event had been planned that evening.

"What social event?" asked the governor.

"Well, one of the prisoners wanted to sell me a ticket for the Warden's Ball."

"That's not a dance, Your Grace, that's a raffle."

WILD LIFE

Why does a male elephant have four feet?

Because six inches would never satisfy a female elephant.

***

Why do hippos make love in the water?

How else can you keep a two tonne fanny wet for two hours?

***

Two old ladies were looking at the giraffe in an enclosure at the zoo. Its arse was at eye level.

"Have a look at its balls!" one said to the other. "I reckon I could squeeze them from here!"

And squeeze them she did.

The giraffe jumped clean out of its enclosure, jumped the zoo fence and was heading for the horizon.

A zoo keeper came up and asked the startled old ladies what had happened. When they told him, he dropped his trousers and said, "You'd better squeeze mine, 'cos I've got to catch the bastard."

WHY OH WHY?

Why do men like to have sex with the light on?

It makes it easier for them to remember your name.

***

Did you hear about the girl who went fishing with five men?

She came home with a red snapper.

***

"Why does that guy in the corner attract all the women?" asked a drinker. "He's not handsome, he's not a flashy dresser, he's not a good conversationalist, he just sits there ... licking his eyebrows ..."

***

Why does Mike Tyson cry after sex?
He's got mace in his eyes.

***

What do you get when you cross a rooster with a jar of peanut butter?
A cock that sticks on the top of your mouth.

XMAS

It was just a couple of weeks before Christmas and the postmaster in the small country town sorted a letter addressed to Santa Claus. He opened it and was touched by its message.

"Dear Santa," it read. "Do you think you could give me $100 to buy a bike? It's not that I want it for myself – it's for my family. My father died last month and my mother has five children and we are very poor. If I had a bike, I would be able to deliver papers so that I could earn money to buy medicine for my little brother."

The postmaster was so touched that he took the letter along to his Rotary meeting and read it aloud to the members. A quick whip-around resulted in $95. The postmaster slipped the $95 into a Rotary envelope, addressed it to the boy and posted it.

The following week the postmaster opened another letter to Santa from the same child. He slipped the envelope into his pocket on his way to Rotary and again, read it aloud at the meeting. It read:

"Dear Santa. Thank you for sending the money for the new bike. Next time you do this sort of thing, be sure not to send it through the Rotary Club as those thieving bastards took $5 commission."

***

Why doesn't Santa have any children?

He only comes once a year – and that's down a chimney.

***

It was Christmas time and the housewife was waiting impatiently at the front gate for the garbage truck. One by one, she took the dustmen to the bedroom and made passionate love to them. Finally, it was the driver's turn, but he was bitterly disappointed when she gave him $20.

"What's this?" he cried.

"For Christmas," she replied. "My husband said, 'give the driver $20 and fuck the rest'."

YES, BUT ...

The captain was on the bridge and there was a heavy fog. He saw a light in front of his ship. He sent a message. "I have right of way."

An answer came from the light. "No you don't. Please turn 30 degrees to port side."

The captain was infuriated. "I'm the captain of a naval ship. Give way," he sent back.

The light answered, "I'm a mariner. Turn 30 degrees to port."

The captain became really angry. "I'm the captain of an aircraft carrier. I will not turn!"

An answer came back. "You'll turn 30 degrees to port side. I'm a lighthouse!"

***

"Sir, I want your daughter for my wife."

"I'm not swapping 'til I see your wife."

***

The middle-aged man was suffering from stress and depression.

"Relax!" was the doctor's advice.

"Do you drink alcohol?"

"No," said the patient, "never touch it."

"There's no harm in a few glasses of wine every night," said the doctor. "Even a cigarette. And have sex, at least once a week. From what you've told me, sex is essential."

Two months later, the patient returned to the doctor, saying he felt much better. He enjoyed a couple of glasses of wine and a couple of cigarettes every night.

"And sex. What about sex?" asked the doctor.

"That's a bit difficult. Only once a month," replied the patient. "I'm the parish priest in a small country town."

YES, OFFICER

The middle-aged couple were driving along the suburban street when the traffic cop pulled them over. "You were doing 95 in a built-up area," said the cop.

"Rubbish!" replied the husband. "I was only doing 60!"

The cop insisted on 95 and the driver was getting very agitated, when his wife leaned over and said, "Don't argue with him, officer. He's always pigheaded when he's had a few drinks."

***

The patrol car pulled over at the scene of the accident, to find a young couple bonking furiously on the side of the road.

"What the hell are you doing!" exclaimed the cop, pulling the girl off the accident victim.

"I was giving him mouth-to-mouth resuscitation," she cried, "when we both got carried away!"

***

The police sergeant told the young constable to clean up the drunks hanging around the local bar.

One drunk walked up to him and asked, "Excuse me, offisser, could you tell me the time?"

"One o'clock," replied the policeman, and hit him once on the head with his baton.

"Christ!" said the drunk. "I'm glad I didn't ask you an hour ago!"

***

The patrol car pulled over behind two motor bikes parked in the scrub at the side of the road. Upon investigation, the cop found two men in the bushes, one with his pants down and the other with his finger up his friend's arse.

"What's going on here?" demanded the cop.

"My mate's had too much to drink. I'm trying to make him sick."

"Well, don't put your finger in there … put it down his throat!" said the cop.

"I'm just about to do that."

***

A driver is pulled over by a police car and the officer asks him to blow in the breathalyser and is asked to show his licence. Upon examination, the police officer says, "You're wearing glasses in your licence photo. Are you long sighted or short sighted?"

"I'm near sighted," said the driver.

"Well, you should be wearing your glasses for driving. I'm issuing you with an on-the-spot ticket for $100."

"But I have contacts!" protested the driver.

"I don't care who you know," said the policeman. "I'm still giving you the ticket."

***

Alec had taken his complaint to the Police Ombudsman.

"I have been persecuted," he complained. "This copper pulled me up in my car and walked around it for twenty minutes looking for some fault and he finally booked me because one of my hub caps was missing. I know that's not an offence."

"What did he book you for?" enquired the Ombudsman.

"Exposing my nuts," replied Alec.

YOU CAN BE STIFF

The roadside sign said, "Rest. Revive. Survive. Arrive", so the motorist pulled onto the side of the road and closed his eyes. He had just got off to sleep when a jogger tapped on his window and asked for the time. The motorist told him it was 6 a.m. He was just getting off to sleep when he was awakened by another jogger who asked the time. "It's 6.30," he growled.

This happened three or four more times, so he wrote a sign and stuck it on his window. It read, **"I do not have the time."** He had just got off to sleep and there was another tap on the window. It was another jogger. "It's 7.45," said the jogger.

***

Xavier was asked how he got his black eye.

"I was teaching my girlfriend the La Bamba when her father came in. How was I to know he was stone deaf?"

***

A burglar had broken into a house, and as he was feeling his way through the darkened room, he heard a voice. "Jesus is watching you!"

The burglar was startled and stood still for a few moments. Then he decided to continue his search for valuables. Once again, he heard the voice, a little louder, "Jesus is still watching you!"

"What's going on?" he thought. He waited a little longer before continuing his search. Again, he heard, "Jesus is watching you!"

The burglar couldn't stand it any longer. He switched on his flashlight, and there, sitting on the perch, was a parrot.

"Was that you talking?" asked the burglar.

"Yes," said the parrot.

"Well, you talk pretty well," said the burglar.

"I've been talking for fifty years," said the parrot.

"You gave me a fright when I came in," said the burglar. "What's your name?"

"Alfred," replied the parrot.

"That's a pretty weird name for a parrot," said the burglar.

"Yeh, but not as weird as 'Jesus' for a rottweiler."

***

Did you hear about the eighty-five-year-old who was acquitted of a charge of rape?

Because the evidence wouldn't stand up in court.

***

Herbie limped into the club to have a few beers with his mates.

"What's wrong, Herbie? You're looking a bit pale," said one.

"Well," said Herbie, looking a bit embarrassed, "I've been in jail for six months after being charged with rape."

"But, mate! You're eighty-five!"

"That's the problem," said Herbie. "I pleaded guilty and I got six months for perjury!"

ZOOS

Little Johnnie was at the zoo with his mum and dad. He had never seen an elephant before.

"What's that thing hanging between its front legs, Mum?"

"That's its trunk."

"And what's that thing hanging between his back legs?"

Embarrassed Mum said, "That's nothing."

Johnnie wasn't happy with this answer and asked his father for confirmation.

"What's that thing hanging between his back legs, Dad?"

"That's his penis," said Dad.

"Mum said it's nothing."

"Yes, but your mother's been spoiled."

***

The female gorilla at the local zoo had become irritable and moody. She was examined by a veterinarian.

"She's in season, and needs a mate," he said.

The zoo manager decided to advertise to get someone to have sex with his gorilla and placed an ad in the newspaper.

"Wanted. A male to have sex with a female gorilla – $10,000."

Next day, Paddy showed up at the zoo.

"I'll make love to the gorilla on three conditions," he said.

"1 I don't have to kiss her.

2 If there's a baby, I won't have to pay support.

3 You'll have to give me a couple of weeks to raise the $10,000."

***

263

Jobs were hard to get but there was a vacancy at the zoo. On arrival, Pat was told that the gorilla had just died and that they wanted him to put on a gorilla suit and pretend to be a gorilla until another one could be found.

Pat began to enjoy his job a great deal. Eating bananas, swinging from branch to branch, entertaining the spectators and lying in the sunshine.

One day, while putting on a performance for a big crowd, he swung a bit too far and landed in the lion enclosure next door. He jumped to his feet when he saw two lions growling fiercely. He ran to the bars, screaming for help. He turned round and faced the lions and one said, "If you don't stop that bloody screaming and shouting, we'll all lose our jobs."

AND FINALLY ...

Why do women fake orgasm?
Because they think men care.

***

Why don't men fake orgasm?
'Cos no man would pull those faces on purpose.

***

A recent survey shows that 36 million American men said that they would never make love to Madonna – again.

***

What does a blonde say after sex?
"So ... do you all play for the same team?"

What's the difference between a blonde and the Titanic?
Only 880 people went down on the Titanic!

***

What's the difference between getting piles and breaking off an engagement to a blonde?
When the piles clear up you get your ring back.

***

How does a blonde get rid of unwanted pubic hair?
She spits it out.

***

Why do blondes wear blouses with thick shoulder pads?
So that men have somewhere comfortable to rest their knees.

***

What does the blonde use for protection during sex?
A bus shelter.

***

Why is it called Rap music?
Because the "C" fell off at the printer.

***

What's the difference between a used car tyre and one thousand used condoms?

One's a Goodyear and the other's a fucking good year.

***

What does the Starship *Enterprise* have in common with a piece of toilet paper?

Both circle Uranus looking for Klingons.

***

Why don't Government employees look out the window in the morning?

Because they'd have nothing to do after lunch.

***

LYN: "If you could sleep with any man, who would it be?"
CHERYL: "I'd sleep with Santa Claus."
LYN: "Santa Claus? He only comes once a year!"
CHERYL: "Yes, but he fills your stocking."

***

How do we know that Jesus was Jewish?

Because he lived at home until he was 30, he went into his father's business, his mother thought he was divine and he thought she was a virgin.

***

Bill went to the doctor complaining of stomach cramps. After diagnosis the doctor told him that he had Terminal Diarrhoea.

"What can you do to help me, doctor?" pleaded Bill.

"Nothing," said the doctor, "it runs in your genes."

***

Jesus stood before the Disciples at the Last Supper and held up a glass of water. "I will take this water and turn it to wine!" he declared.

"No bloody way mate!" yelled St. John from the other end of the table. "You'll put $20 in the centre like the rest of us!"

***

A man called the King Brothers Chinese Restaurant for some food:

"Hello ... King Brothers Restaurant," a man answered.

"Are you Wang-King, the Manager?"

"No ... I'm Foo-King, the Chef."

"Sorry ... I'll call back when you're not busy."

***

MICHAEL: "Hey Carol, if you woke up in the morning with grass stains on your hands and knees, your knickers around your ankles and a used condom on the bed beside you, would you tell anyone?"

CAROL: "Hell, no!"

MICHAEL: "Then how about a picnic tomorrow?"

***

Ben applied for a job as bartender at the local hotel. The owner had heard that Ben had been fired from his last hotel job because he was always late, money was often missing from the till and it was rumoured that he was gay.

"I'll give you a chance," said the new employer, "but if there's any money missing or you're late you will be fired immediately. Now give me a kiss and get to work."

***

In a child custody case the judge took the unprecedented step of allowing the child to decide his own future. "Do you want to live with your father?" he asked.

"No," replied the child, "he beats me all the time."

"Well, do you want to live with your mother?"

"No," said the child, "she beats me too."

"Well, who do you want to live with?" asked the judge.

"I want to live with the English Cricket Team," replied the child, "they never beat anyone."

***

It was Bill's first day in the prison lunchroom. A guy at the next table stood up and shouted "Number 39!" Everyone burst into laughter. A guy at the table behind him stood up and shouted "Number 324!" Again they cheered and clapped. A guy on Bill's table stood up and called out "Number 91!" and everyone giggled and clapped again.

"What's going on here?" Bill enquired of one of the other inmates.

"It's joke-telling time on Tuesdays," he said, "but we've only got one joke book in the prison library and we've all read it, so rather than making us hear the jokes over and over we just call out the numbers. If everyone likes the number they clap or laugh."

Another prisoner stood up and called "Number 184!" but no-one laughed. "Number 628!" he yelled, but still

268

noone laughed. "Number 474!" he mumbled. The prisoners began to shout at him and told him to sit down.

"What happened to him?" asked Bill.

"Well," said the fellow inmate, "some people can tell 'em and some people can't."

***

Luigi was given the job of painting the ceiling of the local Catholic church. He had been lying on his back on the scaffolding for two weeks and it was becoming boring. One morning he saw a big·fat Italian woman enter the church dressed in black. She knelt at the statue of Virgin Mary and began to pray. Luigi decided he'd have a bit of fun. "Hey you down here," he yelled, "this is Jesus Christ talking to you in person!"

The Italian woman stopped praying and looked up to the ceiling where the voice came from. "Hey you upa there!" she screamed, "shudduppa you face – I'ma speaka to your Mudda!"

***

Luigi heard that if you speak to the Virgin Mary you can get anything you want in life. He decided he wanted a new bike, so he wrote a letter to Virgin Mary promising to say his prayers every day. But no bike arrived. So he wrote a second letter and asked Virgin Mary again for the bike. He promised not only to say his prayers but to take the garbage out twice a week. But still no bike appeared. He wrote a third letter asking again. This time he promised he would take the garbage out, do his homework and help little old ladies across the road. But still no bike appeared. He decided to write a final letter. He sat at his father's desk, took the cross of Jesus off the wall, put it in a drawer, locked it with the key and wrote the following letter – "Dear Virgin Mary, if you ever want to see your son again ..."

***

What's the difference between cheating on your wife and cheating on the taxman?

If you get caught, the taxman will still want to screw you.

***

Bill was seventy-five years old when he decided to take up walking. He began by walking five kilometres every day and soon he was in such great health that he had the body of a fifty-year-old. He met an old friend who said, "Bill, I didn't even recognise you – you look fantastic." This encouraged Bill to join a health club, so he started walking five kilometres a day and working out at the gym 4 days a week. Soon he had the body of a 40-year-old. One day at the gym he met an old girlfriend who said, "Bill, you look fantastic! I didn't even recognise you!" He was so inspired by this he joined a singles club and began disco dancing 3 nights a week plus working out at the gym plus walking five kilometres a day. Six months later he had the body of a thirty-year-old. He fell in love with a twenty-one-year-old woman and proposed marriage. She accepted. In their honeymoon suite on the eleventh floor of the Hilton Hotel he said, "Darling this is the happiest day of my life. I'm going to jog across to the bottle shop and buy us a bottle of Moet champagne." He jogged eleven floors down to the hotel staircase, straight across the road and was hit by a truck. He was killed instantly and went straight to Heaven. On arrival at the Pearly Gates he approached God and said, "Why did you do it, God? Why did you take me now? It was the happiest day of my life!" God looked at him and said, "Bill, is that you? I didn't even recognise you! You look fantastic!"

***

Terry joined the army and was terrified about having to make his first parachute jump. On the day of the jump he told his wife that he couldn't do it but she reassured him and sent him off for the jump. On his return she asked him how it went.

"Dreadful!" he said. "When the plane got to 10,000 feet, we lined up for the jump and when it got to my turn I just froze in the doorway!"

"So what happened?" she pressed.

"The sergeant came up behind me, pulled out his huge dick and said that if I didn't jump he'd stick it right up my arse!" said the embarrassed husband.

"Well, did you jump?" she asked.

"Yes – a little bit at first ..."

***

A mean-looking guy takes a seat at the bar. He's 6' 6", has tattoos all over, earrings in his nose and a scarred face. He turns to the guys sitting on his left and says, "All the guys on this side of the bar are motherfuckers! Anyone got a problem with that?"

He turns to his right and yells "All the guys on this side of the bar are cocksuckers! Anyone got a problem with that?"

Noone wants to mess with this guy so they ignore him. A man on the left side of the bar walks towards the tough guy.

"What's your problem?" demands the tough guy.

"I'm on the wrong side of the bar."

***

How do you confuse an archaeologist?

Give him a tampon and ask which period it's from.

***

What do men say when they play hide-and-seek or have sex?

Coming, ready or not.

***

God spoke to Adam. "Adam, I have good news and bad news. The good news is that I will give you two organs to give you great power and pleasure. I will give you a brain to enable you to think and to control the world. And I will give you a penis to give great pleasure in lovemaking."

"Sounds great, God!" said Adam. "But what's the bad news?"

"You only have enough blood to work one at a time."

***

A little girl was telling Santa what she wanted for Christmas and as she listed one thing after another she said, "... and I want a G.I. Joe and Barbie, and ..."

"But Honey," Santa interrupted, "you mean you want a Ken and Barbie?"

"No, Santa!" she said. "I want a G.I. Joe and Barbie!"

"But Barbie comes with Ken!" Santa insisted.

"No!" the little girl exclaimed. "Barbie comes with G.I. Joe! She only fakes it with Ken."

***

An eskimo was riding his snowmobile when it broke down. He got off, and noticed a gas station nearby. He went over, got the mechanic and brought him over to the machine. The mechanic bent down, fiddled with the motor, looked back up and said to the eskimo, "I think you just blew a seal."

"No," said the eskimo, "that's just frost on my moustache."

***

WHO'S THE BOSS?

When God made man, all the parts of the body argued over who would be boss. The brain explained that since he controlled all the parts of the body, he should be boss. The legs argued that since they took the man wherever he wanted to go, they should be boss.

The stomach countered with the explanation that since he digested all the food, he should be boss. The eyes said that without them, man would be helpless, so they should be boss. Then the asshole applied for the job. The other parts of the body laughed so hard that the asshole became mad and closed up. After a few days the brain went foggy, the legs got wobbly, the stomach got ill, the eyes got crossed and unable to see. They all conceded and made the asshole boss. This proves that you don't have to be a brain to be boss ... just an asshole.

TASTELESS JOKES

What's the similarity with a mobile telephone and a clitoris?

Both turn on with the touch of a finger and every cunt's got one.

***

If the bird of peace is the dove then the bird of true love is the swallow.

***

A woman went to the doctor with an unusual problem.

"Doctor, I've got three breasts," she declared.

"Please undress," said the doctor.

"Doctor, I'm worried that when you see my problem you'll laugh," she said nervously.

"Don't be concerned, Miss," said the doctor, "I'm a medical man and I'm fully trained to handle such problems."

She took off her blouse revealing her three breasts and the doctor burst into uncontrollable laughter. So she lifted her arm and pissed in his face.

***

What's the definition of Eternity?

It's the time between when you come and she goes.

***

What's the difference between an Irishman and a trampoline?

You take your boots off before you jump on a trampoline.

***

What's the difference between BSE and PMT?

One is Mad Cow's Disease and the other is an agricultural infection.

***

Ray, the local stationmaster, was having a beer at the pub with his mates. "I had an incredible experience last night," he said. "I saw something lying on the tracks so I went to investigate. I found a woman who had tied herself to the tracks!"

"So what did you do?" asked his mates.

"I untied her and took her back to my place and made a strong cup of coffee. Then I poured a couple of drinks, put on some soft music, one thing led to another, and I finished up having the wildest night of sex I've ever had!" he bragged.

"Was she good looking?" asked a drinker.

"Dunno," said Ray, "I couldn't find her head."

MALE CHAUVINIST JOKES

Why did God give men penises?
So they'd have at least one way to stop a woman talking.

***

What's the difference between a pay cheque and your dick?
You don't have to beg a woman to blow your pay cheque.

***

What's it called when a woman is paralysed from the waist down?
Marriage.

***

What are the small bumps around a woman's nipples?
It's Braille for "suck here".

***

What's the difference between a woman with PMS and a Rottweiler?
  Lipstick.

***

If your wife keeps coming out of the kitchen to nag you, what have you done wrong?
  Made her chain too long.

***

Why are hurricanes normally named after women?
  When they come they're wild and wet, but when they go they take your house and car.

***

Why did the army send so many women with PMS to the Gulf War?
  They fought like animals and retained water for four days.

***

Why is a fat woman like a skateboard?
  They're both fun to ride, but you wouldn't want your friends to see you on either.

***

What's the best thing about a blow job?
  Seven minutes silence.